The Selected Poems of

YANG WAN-LI

The Selected Poems of
YANG WAN-LI

TRANSLATED BY

David Hinton

SHAMBHALA

Sʜᴀᴍʙʜᴀʟᴀ Pᴜʙʟɪᴄᴀᴛɪᴏɴs, Iɴᴄ.
2129 13th Street
Boulder, Colorado 80302
www.shambhala.com

Cover Art: "Boats to the Door" by Shitao, 1656–1707.
Cover Design: Daniel Urban-Brown
Interior design: Steve Dyer

9 8 7 6 5 4 3 2 1

Fɪʀsᴛ ᴇᴅɪᴛɪᴏɴ
Printed in the United States of America

Shambhala Publications makes every effort to print on acid-free, recycled paper.
Shambhala Publications is distributed worldwide by Penguin Random House, Inc., and its subsidiaries.

Lɪʙʀᴀʀʏ ᴏF Cᴏɴɢʀᴇss Cᴀᴛᴀʟᴏɢɪɴɢ-ɪɴ-Pᴜʙʟɪᴄᴀᴛɪᴏɴ Dᴀᴛᴀ
Names: Yang, Wanli, 1127–1206 author | Hinton, David, 1954– translator
Title: The selected poems of Yang Wan-Li / translated by David Hinton.
Description: Boulder, Colorado: Shambhala Publications, Inc, 2026. | Includes bibliographical references
Identifiers: LCCN 2026007149 | ISBN 9781645475002 trade paperback
Subjects: LCGFT: Poetry
Classification: LCC PL2687.Y3 S45 2026
LC record available at https://lccn.loc.gov/2026007149

The authorized representative in the EU for product safety and compliance is eucomply OÜ, Pärnu mnt 139b-14, 11317 Tallinn, Estonia, hello@eucompliancepartner.com.

CONTENTS

CONTENTS

II. Second Awakening (1178–1192: Age 50–65)

CONTENTS

CONTENTS

CONTENTS

CONTENTS

INTRODUCTION

AT THE VERY HEART OF THINGS is the eye. Yang Wan-li's poems couldn't be much simpler—but at the same time, they contain remarkable depths. And those depths begin with that eye at the heart of things. Our modern scientific account of the eye goes like this: The Cosmos evolved our planet and eventually water. Soon, in hollows on the planet's primeval surface, mirrored pools and lakes appeared. There in those pools and lakes, the Cosmos turned toward itself for the first time on this planet. It became "aware" of itself, "awakened" to itself in that mirrored opening deep as all space and light, deep as the visible itself. Eventually, the Cosmos evolved image-forming eyes, and it was awakened to itself once again, conjuring its vast dimensions as the opening of consciousness inside sentient beings like us. At the very heart of things is the eye, and Yang Wan-li returns over and over to this elemental eye and its gaze:

it's this lake's mind—that gaze holding the mountain utterly.

this river's mind: a single eye limitless in all four directions.

Or, turning to his own gaze:

leaving a lofty pavilion to exhaust depths of sight,
I climb this mountain into horizon-wide clarities.

With the eye, in ancient China, came landscape: literally, in classical Chinese, "rivers and mountains." Rivers-and-mountains landscape captivated the eyes of artist-intellectuals and gave rise to their arts and philosophy. Yang Wan-li (1127–1206 C.E.) lived during the Sung Dynasty (960–1279), the age when China's tradition of breathtaking rivers-and-mountains painting was at its height. As if a prophecy, Yang's given name, *Wan-li*, means "ten thousand miles." Yang spent his life as a government official frequently assigned to far-flung posts around the country, and this required extensive travels among China's rivers and mountains. From that prophecy fulfilled came Yang's distinctively original poems, for they were written during his travels between those posts, travels that involved intense and often lengthy immersions in landscape. Even when he was comfortably settled in place and working at his governmental duties, his poems are often built around landscape. And when, at the age of sixty-five, Yang finally retired from this grueling life and settled in his ancestral village (Part III of this book), the poems retained that sense of movement and landscape. Mountains appear by the thousands in Yang's poems, by the tens of thousands. Yang hikes amid those mountains and wanders the rivers veined through them, like the inconspicuous figures in those magisterial rivers-and-mountains paintings, figures who seem to belong so wholly to those landscapes that they nearly vanish into them. Yang's poems reveal the challenges of such belonging—the existential exposure to difficult weather and unknown places, dangerous river gorges and rapids, exhaustion and hunger, etc.—but through it all, that elemental eye is always at the heart of his travels and his poems.

The political situation in China was fraught. In the year of Yang's birth, tribal nomads invaded and occupied northern China. The government fled to a new capital in the south, where there was constant infighting over the proper response to this occupation of the north: appease the "barbarians" with deference and payments, or attack and try to retake the north. In addition, there were internal rebellions, frequent border skirmishes, and failed military campaigns trying to reclaim the north. Yang spent his life as a devoted and quite successful government official, holding a number of high-level positions like provincial governor and advisor to the emperor. As such, he was very much involved in those intrigues—once even leading government forces to put down a local rebellion. This brought him the rewards of social influence, prestige, and salary, but also at times the considerable personal costs of ostracization, demotion, and even exile. And it is said that, in the end, the seventy-nine-year-old Yang died of grief when he learned that a military campaign to retake the north had failed disastrously.

Through it all, however, Yang's kept his poetic practice separate from his political life. His was a poetry of spiritual self-cultivation, rivers-and-mountains poetry shaped by Ch'an (Zen) Buddhist insight—and it made him quite famous as a poet in his time. Not only is that elemental eye and its depths at the heart of Yang's poems, it is also at the heart of Ch'an. Although Ch'an provided the fundamental framework for all Chinese poetry, Yang probably had a more thoroughly Ch'an conception of poetry than any other major poet in the tradition—though not in a doctrinal way that would limit his broad appeal as a poet. The purpose of Ch'an meditation is to empty mind of all our conceptual structures, including self-identity itself, returning us to that opening of consciousness that the Cosmos originally conjured in us. Once that empty-mind dwelling is established, perception is a spiritual act, the eye a mirror reflecting the ten thousand things of this world with perfect clarity: inside become outside, and outside inside. Hence, a mind that is elemental and crystalline as a mirror-deep lake or still river:

it's this lake's mind—that gaze holding the mountain utterly.

this river's mind: a single eye limitless in all four directions.

This empty-mind puts the eye again at the heart of things, as the Cosmos gazing out at itself. It is the essence of Ch'an awakening, and Yang Wan-li returns to it again and again.

Yang's Ch'an conception of poetry begins with his formation as a poet. He studied and imitated the poetic masters of the past assiduously—trying to map his mind onto theirs, to plumb their wisdom all the way down, and to match his poetic insight to theirs. All poets do this, in some sense, but Yang conceived it as a Ch'an practice, an adept practicing under Ch'an masters. He even spoke of those poets as sangha-cases (koans), the conundrums that Ch'an students were assigned to resolve. One of the most essential teachings of sangha-cases and Ch'an more generally is self-reliance and freedom from teachers. Hence, for Yang to resolve those sangha-cases was to overthrow the master-poets of the past—to become his own person and begin writing original poetry, trusting his own poetic responses to his own immediate experience. Yang conceived this crucial event as a poetic awakening experience, and his came at the age of thirty-five (Part I of this book), when he burned all of his poems (over a thousand) and began anew, writing in his own voice.

His own voice, and yet still working within a tradition that was by now almost eight hundred years old, a tradition of poetry that was essentially Ch'an in nature, and based on the awakening of that elemental eye's mirror-deep gaze. It is a poetics of immediate personal experience, based on striking clarities of precise images (the distractions of metaphor and literary embellishment are rare), most essentially rivers-and-mountains landscape images, but also images of everyday things at hand. Hence, a remarkably simple poetry, and a poetry that renders in its very form the immediate experience of Ch'an empty-mind, that foundational integration of self and landscape that was the essence of awakening or sage dwelling for Ch'an practitioners. As this is the fabric from which Chinese poetry was made, that poetry is always already awakened in its very nature. And there is no better exemplar of this than Yang Wan-li. Yang wrote many poems made of nothing more than a crystalline attention to things themselves: sometimes the most ordinary things—a fly, for instance, sunning on a windowsill (p. 46)—but more often dramatic rivers-and-mountains landscape, that clarity of mirror-deep seeing during his extensive travels through

China's rivers and mountains. And his favored form is the short quatrain, ideal for distilled crystallizations of perception.

Yang Wan-li's landscape practice of mirror-deep seeing is part of a broader poetic practice that he called 活法. The common meaning of 活 is "living, lively, active," or "to enliven, bring to life." And 法 means "dharma," the way of Ch'an teaching and practice. So, the straightforward meaning of 活法 poetry is "a poetry that brings dharma to life," "living-dharma" poetry that enacts Ch'an insight. And what this meant first of all was strategies to awaken mind to its empty mirror-deep nature: simple everyday language and content, imagistic clarity and startling moments of visual surprise, twists of humor and whimsical flights of imagination, improvisational and associative leaps, illusion and paradox and mysterious transformations.

Yang describes himself as having a second awakening experience at the age of fifty (Part II of this book), one that reflected the deeper philosophical dimensions in his 活法 poetry that becomes apparent when we attend to the original etymological meaning of 活 and the more fundamental Ch'an definition of *dharma* (法). From the idea that awakening is that empty mirror-deep mind, that elemental eye at the heart of things, comes *dharma*'s most fundamental meaning: the sheer thusness of things that is the most profound teaching. But this thusness is not reality as a static assemblage of things, as we tend to conceive it, but reality as a generative tissue in constant transformation. The ancient Taoist term for this tissue is Tao (Way), and the term continued central in Ch'an. A standard image for understanding Tao is moving water, for Tao moves like water: selfless, effortless, relentless, and in constant transformation. This returns us to the more fundamental meaning of the etymological elements in 活: "water" + "tongue/sound" 氵, stylized and abbreviated form of 川, image of streamwater flowing + 舌, stylized picture of a mouth with tongue emerging). Hence, the "sound of water," from which comes the term's common meaning of "living, alive," etc.

Seen at this level, then, "living-dharma" becomes "flood-thusness." And to practice flood-thusness in poetry or life is to move freely with the fluid spontaneity of Tao (our Cosmos), the effortlessly unfurling Great Transformation of the ten thousand things. Complementing mirror-deep seeing, this water-like movement is the second fundamental aspiration of Ch'an—the two together leading to the overall goal of dwelling as integral to the living Cosmos. And this spontaneous movement becomes central to Yang Wan-li's poetics.

Yang's second awakening recognizes the movements of thought as movements of Tao or dharma, and that realization led to an enormous poetic output. He wrote about 750 poems in the fifteen years between his first awakening and second (ages 35 to 50), but wrote 500 in just the first year after this second enlightenment event, then another 3,000 during the twenty-eight remaining years of his life (over 100 poems per year): a remarkable total of around 4,250 poems. This represents the full realization of Yang's flood-thusness poetics because he was writing as Tao, poetic thought moving the way the Cosmos moves, with the same selfless spontaneity.

In addition to being the height of rivers-and-mountains painting, the Sung Dynasty was the second great age of Chinese poetry—following after the poetic renaissance of the T'ang Dynasty (618–907)—and Yang is one of its acknowledged masters. That selfless spontaneity gave Sung poetry its distinctive feel vis-à-vis the T'ang: an easygoing, even bland artlessness. It must be said, however, that this anti-poetic approach led to a great many unremarkable poems, and this was certainly true of Yang Wan-li's capacious output. Paradoxically though, this artless poetics means that the most successful poems may be the most unremarkable poems, those that strive least for dramatic or profound effects, but instead simply move as Tao. And indeed, many of Yang's poems do little more than report the facts at hand, feeling like reportage or travelogue. This reflects a typically Sung belief that small effects/gestures are the largest and wisest. But however philosophically interesting such poems may be, they are usually unsatisfying as poems. For that reason, only occasional examples are included in this selection.

Yang also made "flood-thusness" the defining shape of his poetic career, which he described as a perpetual series of transformations in style. This is not, however, reflected in the poems themselves. After Yang's first poetic enlightenment experience gave rise to a poetry of his own, his poems develop and mature, but they remain quite consistent through all of his supposed transformations. This suggests that Yang's awakening in the broader and more fundamental Ch'an sense preceded or coincided with that first poetic enlightenment, and that it remained steady through his life. His second poetic awakening, then, was simply a moment when his Ch'an insight transformed his poetic practice: Although it led to more prolific production, it did not change the nature of Yang's poems. Nevertheless, Yang's self-mythologizing reveals his philosophical commitment to dwelling as an integral part of the perennial transformation of things. In fact, this belonging appears most clearly in the sheer number of poems Yang wrote, recording as they do the ever-changing moments in the life of that mirror-deep eye wandering rivers-and-mountains landscape, wild landscape as a sage presence centering the eye at the very heart of things.

I

FIRST AWAKENING

(1162–1177 C.E.: Age 35–50)

At Hundred-Household Ferry

1

This far from the city, goings-on are quiet in mystery.
Halfway across Appearance River, I see fishing boats,

fishermen trying to drive fish into nets. And I know
only a bustling frenzy of spring robes, nothing inside.

4

A little clear sky, a little rain: road dry, then wet again.
Half pale, half dark: mountains rise ridge beyond ridge.

Among fieldgrass spreading away, I see water-buffalo
backs. Then where rice-starts thin, people's footprints.

Cliffs Along the Road Flaunt an Inky and Ancient Winter-Plum Where One Magpie's Settled on a Branch for the Night—Head Pulled In, Eyes Half Closed

Skewed branch glutted with wind and snow,
sparse blossoms glazed jade-pure with ice:

a magpie endures that cold clarity, perfectly
alone and dear friends with origin-dark quiet.

Inscribed on a Wall at Abbot Lumen's Mountain-Welcome Terrace

In Ch'an's isolate quiet, we're done living sick at heart,
but who passes through Ch'an's gateway to realization?

This mountain amid clouds is the precept. Wanting your
Buddha-deep eye's clarity whole, just bow and ask here.

*For Abbot Lumen, Poet-Monk from East Monastery Who
Came Searching for Me at Pervading-Radiance Monastery*

Old friend, you live deep among white-cloud mountains,
winter-plums, content to simply reveal things happening.

I was standing alone, year's-end, gazing deep into peaks.
Suddenly, after struggling through mud with your horse,

you arrived—and turning, I found three years vanished.
Our eyes are sick, but seeing each other opens laughter,

and we speak with the thusness-clarity of Tu Fu reborn.
Then, no need for words, we share such emptiness again.

*They Give High Officials Fancy Thatch Raincloaks: I Give
Mine to a Pilgrim-Monk Stuck Here Because of Rain*

You come finding no Ch'an stillness, no eyelids peeled away
to awakened sight. And pilgrims can't buy the lavish clarity

wine gives eyes. But here, take this raincloak, go wandering
out beyond rain and gulls in flight, all those rivers and lakes.

Farewell to a Thatch-Hut Mountain Monk

Journeys exhaust a thousand, ten thousand mountains
all thusness-clarity. You fathom their exquisite nature,

green-azure and crow-black mystery. I'm done asking.
Now, this gaze into mist and cloud is itself sage arrival.

*With Noble-Quiet and Season-Perpetua, I Hike to
Universal-Completion Monastery, Then Return Late,
Sailing Across West Lake*

1

The boat's window-screen is too thin to hide clear skies.
My tireless staff wants another walk. It's time to return,

but lakeside mountains have gracious plans to keep me,
distant dharma bells silent, sound itself as yet unknown.

2

Our boat in mist angles off willow shores, cloud mountains
appearing and disappearing among leaves. Then we're clear.

What makes drifting across a lake like climbing a mountain?
It's this lake's mind—that gaze holding the mountain utterly.

3

West Lake is ancient, and yet still sustains us. Who needs
ten miles lavish with crimson blossoms? There's the city

radiant with late light amid inky water all thusness-clarity
depth, tattered waterlilies, broken reeds, frost-tinged wind.

4

The distant city meanders, wrapped in shadowy kingfisher-greens.
At dusk, slant-light splinters through lakewater ripples and swells.

Skies cold, sun sunk away, travelers grow scarce. Alone out here
between far shores, boat light, we skim home into stars scattering.

Following the Rhymes of Assistant-Magistrate All-Gather's Landscape, Skies Clearing After Rain

Autumn floods have cascaded away into winter,
but it's warm, plums already radiant in bloom.

Forest mists ignite, then smolder toward dark.
Geese climb wind, then set out for southlands.

Growing old, is there any sorrow we'll avoid?
Already nothing left, no laziness, no industry,

I'll take a wild shovel to these thousand peaks,
scatter them with sun and moon—lit and free.

First Winter Cold

This fierce cold: who does it attack?
It knows I pawned my warm robes,

and sends dusk birds to delight my
eyes. I'll never get back home now.

*After Descending a Small Stream, Our Boat Drifts Out
onto the Yangtze's Vast Waters*

Boat light as a leaf, we cascade down a mountain stream,
then our stream runs head-on into the Yangtze. Suddenly,

everything goes still, perfectly still. No one says a word.
Just the hush of waves, waves and the beginning of rain.

*Early Summer, Dwelling in Idleness, I Wake from a
Noon Nap*

Sour plums at lunch leave my teeth feeling all feathery.
Banana trees cast green across gauze window-screens.

A long day. I wake from a noon nap empty of thought,
all idleness, watch kids catch falling willow blossoms.

*Sent to Be Inscribed on the Shrine Wall at Lumen-
Origin's Empty-Center Pavilion*

Pavilion in jade-azure gardens among kingfisher-greens:
when will I see kindred depths in its burl-gnarl bamboo?

I hear there aren't many sage-masters in all this beauty,
just a thousand, or maybe ten thousand mountain peaks.

Mid-Autumn Festival: Rain Clearing, the Moon Appears

Rain rinses this world of drifting dust clean, and then
crystalline wind sweeps away seething ruins of cloud:

so begins the grand and wondrous mid-autumn affair.
Luminous moon utterly alone, my one kindred-spirit:

it shines through the eight directions. Residue remains,
a thousand lost ages fresh again in its clarity: no sleep,

no concern, then dawn light joining in. Drunk, I'm all
thusness-clarity itself answering that isolate radiance.

*1st Moon, Fire Year of the Boar: Evening Sky Suddenly
Clears, So I Take a Walk*

Sky suddenly clear, I hop off the wood-cart and set out.
My straw shoes whisper like sand, step after step, until

I face a wildland pond. There's no one, just two ducks
drifting and diving in such luminous depths of the eye.

*At the Capital in Late Spring, That Lost-Traveler
Feeling on a Small Tower at No-Sorrow Inn*

Eyes sick, I happen into books and dare not open them.
I tell friends to avoid the spring mud, and no one visits.

How will I ever get through another long day? I could
circle along this tower railing, a hundred times around.

On the Road Between Towns, We Take a Quick Rest-Stop

Sun low, we haven't yet reached the river town. Slant-light
ignites houses in this valley gone white with mountain mist.

Autumn wind is perfectly enlightened, but not very clever,
trying to adorn itself with the rouge of shoreline blossoms.

Late Autumn, Lake Vast

Mist blown beyond this crystalline emptiness,
dwellings remain amid ten thousand flecks of

wild autumn color. I watch them meticulously
scatter across lake-lit gate after gate after gate.

Wandering at Twin-Scarp

After frost, cold streams unfurl clarities deep beyond clarity,
streamwater looking precisely like ice, ice like streamwater.

Poverty perfected until nothing remains, I come all idleness
wondering only about plums: are they blooming here, or not?

Black Butterfly Above Incense-Lamp Flame

It's dined on blossom stamens, sipped dew for wine.
Now, robes cut thin from black mist and purple frost,

it comes and goes, fluttering circles around the lamp.
It never dreamed there could be this much fragrance.

Autumn Morning, Out Beyond Town

1

Day begins. It's cold again. Among mists flush with dawn
light: river scraps shimmer, mountain tatters, a few houses.

Golden cherries appear, each half-covered in crimson frost,
and white as snow, an absolute river of buckwheat blossom.

2

Wild chrysanthemums topple together here, frost-clotted,
bidding farewell to their icy fragrance on shoreline wind.

A year's bounty crumbles away. All that remains of sage-
masters are a few chickens cackling and that barking dog.

Inscribed on a Wall at Absolute-Meaning Pavilion

1

On a cliff-edge above the lake, terraces and windows wide-
open: we all need a lookout like this to read ancient books.

This pavilion is new, but already a place of age-old insight.
Come. It's lovely exacting such windblown-mist instances.

2

When T'ao Ch'ien saw what it all means, he forgot words.
His *thusness* was place, and today it's taught by this place

here. If someone stops by to ask about thusness-meaning,
it's easy: face in depths of mirror, sky in depths of water.

Eyes Old, I Give Up Books: A Lament

Grown old, I can't decipher books anymore.
Blur is blooming across my eyes. That's that.

Near death, ink lines are enemies, not friends.
Here at this far edge of life, wine's the thing.

After snow, that blade of frost is fiercer still,
and wind's wild chant knocks my hat askew.

My little kids think I'm lazy. They taunt me,
shouting their reading lessons into the night.

*After a Poem by My Prajna-Brother, Elder
River-Crossing*

When talk goes dark in the oblivion of night's
forgetfulness, I'm okay pouring cups too fast.

Not much patience for all those sage-masters,
I've grown kindred to places of wild wonder,

abiding in the landscape of poems, that earth-
altar, and dwelling in the family of all things.

Facing wine alone, free of precepts, why look
deep into thusness itself, that clarity-absolute?

Spring Days

1

Distant sun follows sky away. Slant-light
ignites trees. I look and look. Dogs know:

bark exactly where they themselves bark.
By now, I've wandered half the mountain.

2

It's spring. No wine, but I'm still drunk,
wandering outlands, not asking the way.

Where is azure-deep sky? Brilliant birds
vanish there into emptiness all Absence.

*After Another Poem by My Prajna-Brother, Elder
River-Crossing*

Navigating the year without seeing each other,
we couldn't trade letters too often. You're my

prajna-brother, but after scheming to see you,
I wonder what this person facing me could be.

It's clear as we talk that, of friends all far off,
only you are kindred. And soon drunk, saying

nothing, we gaze deep into this wild thusness
within drunkenness itself, this clarity-absolute.

Year's-End, I Set Out Beyond the City

A warm spell is melting winter snows away,
so I rush out, a crazed clown. My whole life

walking, feet blistered as silkworm cocoons,
and now I've got sun-bleached silk for hair.

Mountains etching bones into remnant frost,
plums tracing branches across watery depths:

I hate endless winter, all that isolate silence,
even if it is the depths of origin-dark wonder.

Nightfall, Standing on the Stone Bridge at Prajna-Lumen Monastery

Boats on the still mirror vanish into banks of mist. Prajna-Lumen sits among willows, deep in this lake's very mind.

Night's shadowy black about to come, me about to leave:
we're like South Mountain and North, two towering peaks.

Living in the Mountains at South Creek, I Wake on an Autumn Day

In the dream, I'm a wind-buffeted monk, hat tumbling away.
I start opening a book, eager to discover some Buddha-truth,

but a buzzing hornet's plan cuts my nap short. Thief raiding
my inkstone in a sunlit window, it drinks the last drop of ink.

Untitled

24

I happen to hear wings beat in pine treetops
and realize it's a beach gull come for the night.
Keep quiet, I whisper to my kids,
afraid we'll scare it off,

but after a while, it suddenly breaks into flight,
breaks into flight heading who knows where.
I quit my job! Quit and came home,
I call to the gull!

Climbing to Stone-Crow Monastery

I look back and see I'm above the trees. Mountains grow
small: a single glance holds thousands, tens of thousands.

And otherworldly cliffs tumble breathtaking away below,
forcing me to look up, dizzy fear keeping eyes wide-open.

A little pavilion seems to understand how exhausted I am,
lets my eyes take wing across half a jade-azure mountain,

and climbing to the summit, I gaze up into tranquil mirror.
Lofty peak, lofty monastery, lofty Dharma-Hall: even with

all these roofs blue and gold, a thousand patchrobe monks,
it feels like walking around on the merest tip of a flagpole,

and wandering free here is the liberation of boundless sky,
twenty years navigating that world below perfectly empty.

Watching Farmers Plant Rice

They've had two unbearable years of drought. But this year,
these villages will delight, celebrating harvest. Old farmers

morning after morning fuss over flooded fields, eyes seeing
those kingfisher-green waters turn to clouds of golden grain.

*I Go to Sleep Dead Drunk, but Soon There's Rampaging
Wind, So I Get Up in the Frosty Night and Sit Until Dawn*

After such jade-pure wine, I sober up quickly. Moon low
casting plum-tree shadow: solace here in the third watch.

I resent old eyes all clarity keeping me awake—and then
hear far into wordless sounds of pine, that sage radiance.

Wandering at Day's End, I Follow South Creek

My thatch hut's here beside South Creek.
To the north, on North Mountain slopes,

ten thousand pines cascade to my fence,
and a thousand cliffs rise from my table.

Everyone loves wildflowers in profusion,
but for me, these few are delight aplenty,

and this one hill makes occurrence itself
enough. Not the least longing anywhere.

What is integrity muddy or rinsed clean?
All I need now is the eye's flood of sight:

and here, sky clearing, I somehow arrive,
wandering brimful wilds along this creek,

creek thinned by snow to a thread slicing
crystalline across exquisite expanses, lit.

Laughing together, the kids and I set out
beyond these distances of the eye's gaze.

After Drum-Light's Poem Having Given Up Wine,
I Face Peonies

1

Sick and without companions, I doze in empty mountains,
maybe roam cliffs, icy friends that soothe my fevered eyes.

I sip wine, touch blossoms. These lavish peonies and I: we
talk about old times. They're companions deep as a dream.

2

Caught in old-age and heartbreak, and wanderer's longing,
I need wine to face blossoms this lavish. Once self's gone

and name empty, what good is this world's wild thusness
all clarity-absolute? I'll just offer wine to this life gone by.

Late Spring, Traces of Rain

A bit sober from overnight wine, a bit dead-drunk:
I feel altogether giddy, or sick, and almost no joy.

On the pond's dark depths, gossamer rain. Alone,
leaning over a railing, I watch circles ripple open.

Small Pond

This eye of springwater is silent, so I savor its slight flow.
Tree shadow, lit water: I love this soft liquid of azure sky.

There's dew glistening over a waterlily blossom's needle-
sharp tip, and perched on that, an early-morning dragonfly.

Reading a Book

Reading a book, I don't mind hard work.
When I tire, I close my eyes for the dark,

or better, I roll up the scroll and meditate,
man and book forgetting words altogether.

Then on a whim, I unroll the book again,
and I'm carried to Hundred-Sage Source:

call it *awakening*, and it isn't awakening,
say *dark-enigma*, and it isn't dark-enigma.

In mind's terrain of empty understanding,
that joy primordial and singular emerges,

but whose delight can it be? It isn't mine,
or the Great Transformation's either. All

existence: I've got it all wrong. Fantastic!
Laughing, I toss the book on my cushion.

Sent to Be Inscribed on Blade-Moon's Ice-Water Jar

1

Outside, you see kingfisher-green hills, a thousand peaks,
and inside, drifting its crystalline pool, a moon half bent.

Hold it close, and the rim stretches away for thirty miles:
all that remains is to plant out shoreline willow and lotus.

2

In this jar, crystalline ice. And in the ice, a person. How
could the dust of this world ever gather anywhere here?

I'll come soon, play with watery moon in this pool: face
lit, white hair littered with stars making me young again.

II

SECOND AWAKENING

(1178–1192: Age 50–65)

*4th Moon, 10th Sun, Fire Year of the Rooster: Traveling
to My New Post at Boundary-Ridge, I'm Stalled by
Wind and Stay Overnight at the River's Mouth
Beneath Blue-Oak Scarp*

Cicadas wail on both shores, unbearable. I light a candle,
and grief thins away to silence. Then I sip at wine. Who

is it here in this boat? That grief seemed like mine, but
now there's only a sail and trace of candle-smoke rising.

On Jade Mountain Road

Water clamors everywhere north and south of this village.
Trees cast deep shadow where these streets begin and end.

Confident, certain that it isn't mere beauty, a green-azure
mountain shines steady all day long in azure streamwater.

*7th Moon, 14th Sun: In Boundary-Ridge, on
Lotus-Garden Bridge After Rain, I'm Surprised
by the Cold*

I hear lotus leaves greet wind, see lotus
blossoms fresh after rain, so I drag my

chair onto the bridge and sit. Suddenly,
I'm deep inside a cold mirror's depths.

Cold Night, No Sleep

Snow falls into hair cut short for spring.
Tea sobers a heart drunk on the ancients.

Dream wanders back to this frost-filled
house. A bell rings: it's the moon askew.

Sitting at Night in the Library

Lamps on the yew table hiss in this room of emptiness.
Outside the window, rain clatters on stairs—then stops.

My old chair and meditation cushion deep in darkness,
half asleep, I can hear a child reading ancient histories.

Dawn Chill

Bit by bit the chill eases. Darkness thins into everyday
clarity. I rarely wander spring anymore, but understand

how spring wind can't bear winter desolation. In fond
farewell to me, I soar on a swing, no need for myself.

I Climb at Dawn to My Ample-Sheaves Pavilion

1

After spring rains, winter-plums begin to yellow. Snow-
flake blossoms fill winterberry branches with fragrance.

Why face bitter wind? Look, simply look deep into this
green-azure thicket, and mind feels its own blank chill.

2

Before the rains, all this farmland was nothing but weeds;
but then after the rains, farmers hurried out to work. Now

everywhere in the eye, the eye entire: thirty miles of shine-
water fields, and rice-starts emerald clear to the sky's edge.

Amid Noonday Heat, I Climb to My Ample-Sheaves Pavilion

1

Skies blazing hot, I can't bear it down there in that valley house.
Ch'i breathes fresh and alive at this lofty pavilion, dark-enigma

Absence too. Without autumn frost, these chill-raveled breezes
won't silence cicadas, but they offer this old-timer arrival whole.

4

Suddenly, among blossoms high above lowland willows, gusty
wind kicks up, lovely, and shatters this grief-stricken face into

smiles. I shed clothes on eight-thousand-foot cliffs and lean out
all idleness, watch cloud far south drift on past North Mountain.

Sitting at Sunset in Slumber-Preside Studio

I close the door and sit. Nothing happens,
so I open a window. A breath of cool air

drifts in. Trees shade out late-light glare.
Stone wet with writing-ink glistens azure.

My hand chooses a book of poems, ever
trusting, and I start chanting cautiously,

something like quiet joy unfurling until
heartbreak suddenly catches hold of me,

then I can't keep on, toss the book down
and set out wandering around the room.

Those ancients brooded like mountains,
but my mind moves placid as any river:

I'm altogether unlike them, so I wonder
how they can wound me this easily, then

all that's over. It's just me here laughing.
Lone cicada song hurries last light away.

Sitting at Dawn in My Ample-Sheaves Pavilion

Radiant sun burns through horizon-wide cloud, scatters it
shattered into scraps of mist tumbling out across villages.

And I'm another cloud-scrap drifting empty sky, no more
sage talk about that kingfisher-green gate of distant peaks.

Taking the Juniper Path at Dawn

Rain ends. The forest falls silent, silent. Cold emerging,
wind pierces through to the path. Dawn clarity sharpens.

I wander further and further, then finally there's no one.
When the mountain bird startles away, I too startle away.

***On My Day Off, Dawn Skies Clear, I Try to
Read a Book at Ample-Sheaves Pavilion***

I brought family to Thorn-Bramble Creek,
became governor, and a first year's already

flown by. The house they gave me is lovely,
but there's always some new worry tearing

me apart: if it isn't a sick servant suffering,
it's my kids wailing about who knows what.

When we were poor, hunger made them cry:
at least this autumn, food isn't the problem.

Today, up early, I tuck a book in my sleeve
and, free at last, climb clear to the pavilion.

Traces of frost linger here, stars and moon.
Distances pour in through wide-open walls.

Somehow feverish heat vanished overnight,
and this ice-cold morning feels miraculous:

Still in summer robes of open-weave gauze:
I suddenly awake to my body, old and sick.

Birds far off seem white-clarity butterflies,
and cicada song seems dark-enigma poems;

pine color comes snowing into sight itself,
and waterlily scents freeze my very nature.

Soon, I can't find joy and sorrow anywhere,
then I've left body and all form itself behind.

No idea what's happening up here, the kids
start shouting, calling me down to breakfast.

Ripples on Water

1

A sharp gust catches the pond's surface,
starts a single wisp of smoke sweeping

across: no form, barely even reflection
plundering water and gone, pure flight.

2

They start as smile-wrinkles at the eye,
and then become bamboo-skin streaks.

Barely a gust, and they can't stay put,
weave gauze on across the entire pond.

Sitting at Dawn in Slumber-Preside Studio

Night wind was so faint it couldn't ease my acrid grief away,
but frost fell cold, silent. When sunrise fills the east window,

there isn't a worry anywhere. I bid plum blossoms farewell,
flecks of shadow scattering through every depth of the eye.

Inscribed Playfully on a Rivers-and-Mountains Painting

That boatman is truly the merest bit of flyspeck,
and the boat a tiny orchid on its wispy leaf-blade.

Who knows where they'll anchor tonight, waves
cresting up and seething high as mountain peaks.

A Cold Fly

Chance sight on windowsill: the fly sits warming its back,
rubbing its front legs together, savoring morning sunlight.

Sun nudges shadow closer. But fly knows what's coming,
and suddenly it's gone: *buzz* heading for another window.

At Chuang Tzu's River

Ten miles of emerald ripples and carefree-ease fish, this river,
this human realm's seething swells—it keeps leaving, leaving.

A shoreline egret has already eaten its fill. Nothing left to do,
it stands there in morning light, fussing over its snowy robes.

After Breakfast, I Climb to Pure-Distance Pavilion
47

At this lone pavilion, lakewater opens out
and the path skirting walls wanders away.

Frost-filled forests the kingdom of crows
and ice-fringed banks the home of egrets,

winter sunlight so fierce I shield my eyes:
sage teachings summon us to the *prajna-*

awakening of rivers and mountains alive.
And I'm here, boiling streamwater for tea!

Gazing at Snow

House turned suddenly silver and stairs frosty jasper,
faint gusts trouble my wine, then silence everywhere.

Powder fallen from clouds of chalky dust: how could
powder trickle, etch delicate blossoms of jade-white?

I look for the sun, but it's still hidden among clearing
skies. Then its radiance fills my courtyard, and soon

it's chasing meltwater away. I dip my brush in, write
sage brilliance onto windows against nights to come.

Skies Clear After Snow

Silver stretches three thousand miles distant.
Jasper-frost forests rise ten thousand ridges

beyond ridges. Fresh green tinting clear sky,
hints of red ignite fallen snow. Mischievous

kids bang sticks at icy pillars, start all clarity
itself tumbling off eaves like bits of blossom.

Who needs the insight of ancient poet-sages?
All this jade-white emptiness is poetry pure.

After Horizon-Gather's Poem **Delighting in Snow**

Yang-deep heaven and *yin*-deep earth: sky in a single
snow rinsed it all clean. But hot-springs are freezing,

promise of seed hangs frozen on jasper-frost grasses,
and plum blossoms battered by the cold need warmth.

I set sail out into lit clarity, but soon turn homeward:
who needs lofty views long and clear? Gates closed,

I bow to ancient words, those sage depths. There too
I can see back into the dark-enigma origins of things.

Last Bits of Snow

Last bits of snow in heaps, mountain beyond mountain
all jade-pure elegance of high cliffs and quiet canyons.

How can I reach out with hands of a mountain-Buddha,
gather them up like lit jewels, these three or four peaks?

Crying, My Kids Ask for Food

Living without decent food and clothes, that loving care:
my little ones are used to it now. They're forever hungry.

Morning after morning I hear their cries, and it seems our
cookpot too longs for a new harvest, millet ripe and ready.

Cold Sparrows

A hundred thousand sparrows descend on my empty courtyard.
More gather atop plum trees, chatting with clear evening skies,

and the rest swarm around, trying to kill me with their racket.
Suddenly they all startle away, and there's silence: not a sound.

Ode to Cheese

Like fat, but tasty and sweet and more:
your tongue seems caressed by winds,

then it's jade-white crumbs on a plate
and snow melted away in your mouth.

*Overnight at My Office, I Wake and Sit Through
the Night*

This year, snow covers that war-torn frontier river,
and tonight's bright half-moon won't melt the ice.

I sit alone, all human endeavor still, perfectly still.
One candle lit: red. Two vases full: plum blossoms.

Kids Playing with Ice

The kids lift morning ice off a metal bowl of water,
thread colorful string through to make a silver gong,

then strike it. Jade rings out through trees, its chime
broken when shattering glass clatters on frozen earth.

Moonlit Night, Gazing at Snow

Moon's radiance, snow's color: they're such cold clarity.
Looking at this moon, I soon suspect it's a disc of snow,

and gazing into radiant snow, I'm sure it's moon. Guess
this must be origins—snow and moon one and the same.

Light Rain

Lonely and depressed, words absent, I lean against the door
alone: plum blossoms and light rain, dusk verging on yellow.

Rain drips off the eaves, sad excuse for a sage lofty and free.
Just one drop after another: won't it ever try anything new?

*Watching a Little Boy Gleefully Smash the Ox-Herd and
Spring-Ox Talismans*

He breaks the clay head first. It's how farmers open the new
spring. For luck, they sow their fields with scattered shards.

The spring-ox has yellow hooves and a pair of white horns,
the ox-herd a green raincloak and hat of jade-azure bamboo,

and they forecast that earth's *ch'i*-veins will pulse with rain.
Last year was disaster, but this year will bring lush harvests,

and learning the year won't bring hunger, that boy's thrilled.
When his ox hears about plenty, it worries about staying fat.

Wheat fields will seem clouds, tassels swaying like brooms,
and rice will abound, filling baskets with perfect little pearls.

First they'll plow those broad fields, then start in mountains.
O that poor ox: how will it ever get another moment's peace?

Don't Read Books

Don't read books,
don't chant poems:

read books and your eyes wither until words are bones,
chant poems and every word's vomited from the heart.

People say it's delightful to read books,
they say it's wondrous to chant poems,

but it means lips hissing on and on like autumn insects,
makes you thin and frail, and ravages you with old-age.

Thin and frail, ravaged with age: maybe you don't mind,
but all that racket is pretty annoying for anyone nearby.

That can't compare to sitting still in a studio, eyes closed:
lower blinds and sweep away dust, light fragrant incense,

then listen to wind, listen to rain. They have such flavors.
When you're strong, walk. And when you're tired, sleep.

On a Boat, Gazing into Rain

A boat in rain is good for nothing but sleep. Without
fine landscape to relish, I just long for easy idleness.

Shoreline table stretching away: real mountains are
pretend there, carefully arranged decoration of fruit.

Passing Below the Traverse Mountain Shrine-Tower

I've crossed Orchid Creek here three times in six years,
always as ruins of spring become summer. O how very

touching: this Traverse Mountain, summit shrine-tower
greeting me as I go east, bidding farewell as I go west.

On the Boat, Passing a Market-Town at Dawn

Windows varnished against rain, the world shines in
dry and clear. East wind whirling up, west wind wild:

they shriek across sails, hiss and grate at riverwater.
Our boat-haulers give up and stand around aimlessly,

and deep in rain, the oarsman loses his hat to a gust.
Before we reach it, a market-town's entered the eye.

Shoreline willows nod and bow. This moment whole:
it's a library of sincerity spoken pure, inviting me in.

Breakfast at Noonday-Ascension Mountain

59

These thousand peaks offer the beauties of spring again,
and what do I offer them? Nothing but mounting alarm.

Clouds plunder cragged cliffs where birds sing in trees,
rain swells mountain streams, cascades scattering petals,

and I can't see past thatch roofs, a wisp of kitchen smoke,
but know exactly how starvation will look in this village.

I knew there'd be no meat for breakfast. But they barely
even have bamboo-shoots: two, maybe three wisps each.

Transplanting Rice-Starts

Young child digs rice-starts, father tosses them across,
mother catches them, and elder child plants them out,

thatch rainhats their helmets and cloaks their armor.
Rain's soaked through hats and halfway down backs.

Grandma calls them all in for breakfast, a bit of rest,
but bent to their task, eyes intent, they don't answer.

Those starts are still bare-root, still not bundled up:
just keep all those baby ducks and geese out of here!

Climbing to the Summit of Auspicious-Star Mountain,
I Find It's a Crag Standing Alone with the Inscription
Shooting-Star Mountain

Standing alone on this summit, this jade-azure wander-star,
I wonder when heaven sent auspicious stars shooting down?

Ten thousand peaks tower up in every distance, all rock and
crag and every one its own shade of jade wander-star azure.

At Plenitude Cliffs

Looking up I see silvered-azure cliffs all depth towering
above this Ch'an temple's exquisite valley. At the empty

center of things, eighty thousand feet off a peak, water
cascades, and even one single drop startles mind awake.

Staying Overnight at Spirit-Vulture, a Ch'an Monastery

1

Sweating in summer heat, I make my way into mountains
where frost fills windblown bamboo and snow fills pines.

Or is it just mountain cold opening clarity through bones,
because there's no frost or snow here, and there's no wind?

2

I thought there was rain all night, but today dawns clear.
Then I realize it's the mountain waterfall crashing down.

It flows on into this courtyard stream without a whisper,
returned to the silence where that mountain sound began.

Sick at the Mid-Autumn Festival, I Can't Drink
63

No wind, no rain, and not a cloud in sight: mid-autumn
is exquisite this year, utterly perfect. You can't turn this

wheel of enlightenment once it freezes up. But its jade-
pure hub of emptiness remains open, traceless. I sit here

watching a confusion of kids pretend to drink, mocking
this old-timer. Suddenly I feel half drunk. But only half:

I can carry moon's sage radiance in a winecup's clarity,
but not a winecup's clarity in the moon's sage radiance.

No Longer Sick, I Feel So Old

When I was ill, I forgot all about age,
but now I'm well again, I feel so old.

No one stays hale and hearty forever.
The ruins of age take over in no time:

mountain thoughts freeze cold suns,
autumn light infects withered poems,

and little pines grow heartless, aping
my palsied shake as I chant this poem.

Banana Trees

Seen framed by window and tile eaves, my few banana trees
may lack the snowy landscape a Wang Wei painting conjures,

but they're wide-open and free of sage inscriptions. And it's
winter-solstice, their jade-green all existence-tissue Absence.

The Sound of Pines

Outtalking my poems with its tangled whisper, a pine
summons wind from flanks of the moon. It makes you

sober then drunk too. So I set out circling around this
mountain, search into the sound of ten thousand pines.

Not Sleeping

Darkness themselves, crickets sing all night on and on,
straight through from smoldering dusk to radiant dawn,

like some newborn child's cries. And they're absolutely
mute about the heart of this grand and wondrous affair.

On through the night, a thousand ten thousand sounds
clarified into a few voicing thusness all clarity-absolute:

this   this   this   this   on and on and   *this   this.*
And hey—is there any other sage talk worth pondering?

West Studio, Rising from a Nap

I nap through the clatter of chill rain here at West Studio,
but then cries of bamboo-partridge cut my dreams short.

I open the door, and mountains come jumbling in, romp
wall-to-wall, staining the books all kinds of green-azure.

Overnight Where Rapids Begin, at Wisdom-Sea Monastery

I've spent a lifetime on the road searching for tranquility,
and tranquility's impossible once you go searching for it.

No gates and no walls, this ancient monastery offers only
one single teaching: depths of night turn springtime cold.

On Ten-Thousand Peace Road

Clouds stripped ragged at Jade Peak, late light slants through.
Mud dry on blossom-laden paths, I can take an evening walk.

One ribbon of wind edges warmth into the cold—languorous,
meticulous. Hints of rain, a few drops flashing flecks of light.

On the Boat in Black-Maw Rapids, Full of Fear

In the cliffwall gorge between two mountains, we float
over dragon dens and under painted bridges. I love this

one peak, all sage wonder itself. I linger on, then set out,
and what looked like one peak suddenly becomes three!

Morning on Black-Maw Ridge

Last night, after descending the rapids, my terror ended.
This morning, I climb cliffwalls to this unknown place:

emerald peaks ranged all around, towering up into azure
skies, no trace of people, sage Ch'an books mere trifles.

Decades chasing renown didn't amount to a chicken rib.
And this vagabond life's just sheep entrails spooled out.

But here, I climb to this plum-blossom ridge, gaze north,
and find the peak of Buddhas a far fleck of green-azure.

On a Boat Crossing Farewell Lake

2

All through that hundred-mile gorge, cascades flooded
homes, the most desperate toppled over into riverwater.

Now, ridgeline wildflowers ripple fresh summer greens,
but spring's bloom still lingers in shoreline silver-grass.

3

I pour out a cup or two of emerald wine inside the cabin.
The door swings closed, then back open onto exquisite

ranged mountains: ten thousand wrinkles no one notices,
and every ridge handpicked by the late sun's slant-light.

Passing Drum-Resound Forest in Light Rain

Our boat's sail angling up, we descend this dragon river.
Why talk about a thousand peaks, or ten thousand peaks?

This little troupe of boatmen with their pointed rainhats,
this would make a perfect rivers-and-mountains painting.

Passing Through Thus-Brights Gorge

I look up into azure skies azure through and through.
Never a ripple, the river's glassy skin doesn't waver.

Broad daylight across mountains. Only one surprise:
I suddenly hear it like the first sound, a cuckoo's call.

Morning Rice at Radiance-Gape Village

Anchored now, and grateful for safe passage, we offer our
rice to the river god. And night, O it's a confusion of want:

we start picking grapefruit blossoms, boil a fragrant broth,
fish soggy water-lettuce and river-leek up out of shallows.

I'm done admiring hillside elders who thrive without meat,
but who could harm these monkeys? Soon I'm mud-drunk,

and here beyond Thus-Brights Gorge, land open and clear,
marvelous contentment of mountains turns hunger into joy.

Leaving the Gorge

I resented our slow boat that morning we sailed into this
mountain gorge's maw, and rejoiced when we finally left.

Mountains are always like family sending a traveler off,
and when travels wear you out, it's easy to go back home.

4th Moon, Listening to Cicadas on My Day Off

Deep amid lychee branches, shadow turns summer heat
cool and clear, and early cicadas start singing: one, two.

Blossom dew, willow wind: we never eat our fill. How
wonderful: I study cicada voices that elucidate nothing.

4th Moon, 8th Sun: I Try Fresh Lychee

One fleck of rouge tints its stem-end and spreads
until suddenly its green robes are completely red,

then jeweled purple, skeletal and gaunt as cloves,
flesh white as snow, cold in midday summer heat.

I don't even dare hold this globe of ice—and yet,
with wine, its wind-honey flavor is unforgettable.

This old glutton's dying to wolf down hundreds,
but I'm afraid they'll freeze my insides to pieces.

On a Summer Day

One word always becomes two and more,
and a few frosty hairs soon become many:

I can stop writing, stop explaining myself,
but then how will I pass another long day?

Lychee are ripe, all crimson and wrinkled.
And wine is ready, ripples tinged emerald.

Once I'm drunk, grief simply drifts away,
or if some lingers, it haunts someone else.

Skies Finally Clear, I Wander the West Garden

Tired of life gazing into mountains, I long to leave;
and when I leave, I'm soon dreaming about return.

So what kind of awakening is possible here in this
existence? I look to peach blossoms at nightfall, lit.

Sunrise in a Banana Orchard, Then We Set Out from the Banked Rocks of Yellow-Nest Jetty

Distances pure clarity, drizzling mists drift mountains
here at Yellow-Nest. Water stretches away into empty

skies. We pick plume-grass seed in shallows, cook up
dawn mush, then cut banana leaves to patch our sails.

Boat People

Blessed by those tribal gods with a life on rivers, they
learn from youth how to wander seething whitewater.

Steamed crab for food, they know nothing of our rice,
and with banana-leaf clothes, who needs fancy gauze?

Spring floods came last night, swallowed the sandbar,
and they just send kids out to gather plume-grass seed.

I laugh in grief at my lifetime spent wandering rivers,
but they float home itself on mountains of silver wave.

Fierce Headwinds Force Us to Anchor at Gather-
Home Village for Three Days, Then We Travel
Twenty More Miles

I only came on this journey south to gaze at mountains.
They flash by quickly, and I keep turning to look again.

It isn't headwinds stopping us now. How is it possible
I can see so utterly these ten thousand crag-bare peaks?

Encountering Rain on the Perpetua-Peaks Road, a
Poem to Ease Depression

Leaving the mountains, I can't see a village, but know
there's one nearby: the land here is opening into fields.

I stop and watch massed clouds tumble down to earth,
then look back to find the summits gone up inside sky.

*Morning Light, We Start Down Graveyard
Rapids Beneath Cragged Peaks*

These southern mountains are gorgeous,
but I so easily miss kitchen cook-smoke,

farmers wandering fields and rich work,
and thatch huts alongside deep streams.

These peaks are pavilions for the moon
alone, shorelines the only fishing jetties.

I could rely on gibbons and smoky mist,
but their cliffwalls only churn up waves

seething. Mountains packed close keep
people distant, and that distance makes

mountains wild wonder. My boat leaves
no trace: mountains gallop past my eye

and away. And they're everything I am:
of life gone by, not a trace remains here.

*Sent to Congratulate Pattern-Sustain, Who Just
Attained Enlightenment*

Life is crazy enough, then old age makes it crazier still.
If you sit polishing Ch'an quiet before an incense-stick,

done going in like a farmer to advise the imperial court,
done with ministers and generals, and even sage sutras,

you find dragons roam north and south, and river to sea,
tens of thousands all snarling jade spit and silver fangs.

Heaven and earth were long ago whole, peak and valley,
but it's all strewn vestige now: rocky lake, windy moon.

Evening at the Lychee Dharma-Hall, Gazing Out

1

Announced by chimes here, evening peaks draw the sun in.
Star River breathes out scarves of vanishing cloud. Autumn

courtyard, silence deepening. And in the pines, two moons:
baby cranes all flown far away now, the nest alone remains.

2

Bones sick and autumn wizened, I fear the clarity of night
and that north wind cold and delicate teasing at my robes.

These windows are doubled paper. Nothing gets through
except here beside my books: a few scattered eyes of light!

81

Cooking Breakfast in a Streamside Village

82

Is this a village trailing streamwater away
like a tail? There's a bridge crossing into

confusions of shore-grove bamboo where
three or four houses face two lofty peaks.

And you'd never know winter is far away
now. It's always cold here, even at noon,

making plum blossoms thin but luminous
clarities kindling thoughts, no idea whose.

*Morning Light Before We Set Out Down
Household Creek*

A little plum tree on a mountain road: it's exquisite,
blossoms scattering for no one, opening for no one.

All this delight and grief that no one knows: perfect,
I'll take a branch of bloom, sweep it across my face.

Mountain in Cloud

Spring mist rises out of the valley, scarves of it coming
day after day, piled up into cloud shrouding the summit.

I so adore this peak, how could I leave? I want to begin,
walk around it two or three times, open again, cloudless.

On Seacoast Cliffs at Lake-Brights, Gazing Out to Sea

Blowing from the sea's far corners, this startling wind
rustles earth and smooths away grief etching my face,

and though I'm here in late spring north of the islands,
my eye reaches clear out to the southern sky's far edge.

Where could those waters stretching toward me begin,
and how did these thousand peaks come to settle here?

It's the most marvelous shrine-room: ten million wide-
open miles of misty wave, and one soaring gull, white.

1st Moon, 3rd Sun: Staying Overnight in a Village

I left at the New Year and kept traveling
three relentless days with barely a pause

on sandy roads crossing flat countryside,
those hundred miles flying past my eyes

infused with the joy of things lit at dusk,
or mired in anger at low-tide rock-muck.

But finally reaching open fields, I began
thinking of this village up among clouds

where I could rest. Why hurry a journey?
If you hurry, you won't arrive anywhere.

These three peaks didn't set out far away
and come bounding here like loud tigers:

they just lingered, waiting, and now rock
back and forth, keeping close to my door.

Facing them and finding we're all friends,
I call out for wine, and we help ourselves.

I'm soon drunk, but not them. Forgetting
each other, we see further into each other.

At West Bridge, Unmooring the Boat and Setting Out

I'm a peon. Have they really sent me away
south to north, back west and then out east?

Gibbon cries, moons in cloud-scoured trees,
travel pillows, winds chilling dew-lit boats:

by now, my hair is a forest white in spring,
my face a blue sky that wine never revives.

Done resenting a life of sickness and grief,
I make time-ravaged peaks my only friends.

Inscribed on a Wall at East Temple's Shrine to the South Sea

Gauze mountain like a ten-thousand-stone bell adrift,
seething cloud roams south here like a thirsty dragon:

thunder rushing, lightning flashing, nowhere to hide
and nowhere to escape. Battering this entire seacoast,

it drinks at sea swells, vomits out smolder-red cloud,
then raises its head billowing into a fire god's palace,

pearl shrines and jade pavilions, water-crystal temple,
dawn flags vermilion on days of ten thousand rivers,

and black-azure mountains all around like city walls,
their mountain feet drowned under billowing swells.

I hadn't made this climb to Sundance-Water Pavilion,
but now I come gazing out to sea, and it's terrifying,

all that black-azure like some jade bracelet left open,
wild surf soaring in to batter its way through the gap.

Then suddenly skies clear, a few flecks of snow drift,
and all-beneath-heaven opens to exquisite emptiness,

boundless seas stretching away again east of the bay.
West Temple doesn't have the power of East Temple:

it isn't lofty enough. Only at East Temple can I gaze
clear out into this vast library of ancestral teachings,

delight in the ocean spirit's elegant sutras of stormy
rain clearing. Even out on a terrace wide-open to all

heaven and earth, there's nothing to realize. Sunlight
ignites watery precepts falling off eaves drop by drop.

Boatman Playing a Flute

On this endless river, no wind, the water is glassy green,
not the least leather-wrinkle, or even gauze-weave ripple:

east and west, it drifts incandescence through emptiness,
a thousand miles of flawless jade, its pure luster radiant.

Our young boatman can't bear all this tranquil stillness:
drunk, he grabs a flute, breathes song out beyond cloud,

sound steady and crystalline, carrying clear through sky:
mountain gibbon howling into moon, stream cascading.

The other boatman joins in with a sheep-skin hip drum,
fingers pattering like rain, head like a green-azure peak,

then suddenly, midstream here in this river, a giant fish
shatters crystal-clear water, leaps free and soars ten feet!

Night Rain at Luster Gap

The gorge's river all empty clarity, rain sweeps in,
cold breezy whispers beginning deep in the night,

and ten thousand pearls start clattering on a plate,
each one's *tic* a perfect clarity piercing my bones.

I scratch my head in dream, then get up and listen
till dawn, hearing each drop appear and disappear.

After a lifetime listening to rain, my hair's white,
and I still don't know night rain on a spring river.

Leaving Thus-Brights Gorge

1

Sailing clear of treacherous rocks and seething pools,
I turn to look ahead, and the cragged peaks are gone.

Cold spring, the operations of dark-enigma Absence
still. It's a plaincloth robe. Wearing it, I know myself.

2

Delicate rain arrives, stitching three-needle two-thread
tangles on the river, and there's no confusion. But who

ever fathoms cascades seething into frenzied onslaught,
scattering millions upon millions of wounds and scars?

9

Spring radiance infuses river darkness again. My painted
boat a water-pavilion offering clear-eyed clarity, leaving

Thus-Brights brings regret, a backward gaze. What luck:
I can see peaks the green-azure of bamboo-shoots in rain!

10

Who needs the hunger of all-beneath-heaven, lovely land,
sunlit mountains? It's the emptiness whorled in my bones.

No delicacies to offer ancestors: that's the only regret left
me here, descendent of these cragged Thus-Brights peaks.

*1st Moon, 28th Sun: Watching Swallows Outside
the Gorge*

At the New-Year Earth-Festival, I long for Ch'an stillness
somewhere. The full moon passes, then swallows return,

a pair skimming along the water. So relentlessly elegant:
unable to fly tranquil, they arc through edges and angles.

*After Climbing Three-Road Mountain, a Midday
Nap on the Boat*

Midday, mind gone shadowy dark, I can't stay awake,
so I find a bamboo mat. I'm worn out, but can't sleep,

just blur into wavering dream wondering if it's dream
listening to the sound of people in the sound of water.

Eating Steamed Buns

Perfecting fourfold insight, the sangha steams buns,
offers them in dragon-weave baskets at a crossroad.

An old-timer comes, hungry and not the least serene
wolfing one down like a mountaintop vulture. And I

can't stop: my poet-belly shriveled to a cicada shell,
I gobble buns down hand over fist until, finally full,

I suddenly drop my chopsticks and break into smile,
call out for dragon-coil tea fizzing crab-eye bubbles.

Cottonwood Blossoms

We speak of them cascading down, flutes singing farewell.
Once they fly off, they never think of return. Flooding sky,

they float beyond our control, sheer trace and vestige wind-
blown away. Or they drift into spiderweb, and fly no more.

*1st Moon, 24th Evening: We Call for Wine and Climb a
Small Tower to Watch the Release of Festival Lanterns*

Lofty peaks north and south make eyes drunk without wine.
Soon, market racket grows still as the origin-quiet of recluse

cliffwalls. You talk about rain last year on West Lake. Then
suddenly I hear it there, outside the city, loud on waterlilies.

***On the Road Back to Blade-Moon Monastery, I Gaze
at the Cragged Peaks of Tiered-Anew Mountain***

Windy moon its liver and spleen, icy snow its heart,
masterful adepts chisel emptiness from empty skies

where it soars, ridges cut into mist-and-cloud bone,
peaks purpled kingfisher-green mirage above cliffs.

To see it not as fruit on display, but as itself exactly:
that is illumination. But how can I realize this jade-

pure dragon when I'm grief-torn and hurrying back?
Suddenly, I see slant-light is the evening bell struck.

*Summer Heat Fierce, I Watch the Houseboy Out in
Our Garden Divert Water to Create a Waterfall on
Our Little Make-Believe Mountain*

Out beyond the back eaves, our little crag-rock mountain,
one peak a lone pinnacle, and other peaks crowded close:

suddenly water bursts out on twenty-thousand-foot cliffs
and takes flight, a crystalline cascade of midsummer chill.

It's the houseboy out having fun! He's turned an old well
topsy-turvy, and surprise: a crashing torrent! I'm ancient,

terrified of the intense heat these last few years, and now
relish pearls skittering across the rippled jade of my gaze.

Eating Lotus Seeds

White-jade hornets nestled inside green-jade hornet nests:
cut them free, and they're frosted with dew, taste of wind.

Soaked in a glass bowl of icy wine, they make you drunk,
turn you into a hundred tangles of lotus, fresh and young.

Washing My Face

Waterfold Mountains bid this returning boat farewell along
both shores. Spring's freshly-ground indigo tints sky-azure

river shallows. I dip water out, rinse mouth and face clean,
morning crystalline, this face fragrant as a falling blossom.

After Passing Mutual Gap, We Approach Bend Lookout

Rising from a nap, my robes are a crumpled mess
and my cap is battered with hundreds of wrinkles.

Sail wrapped tight to the mast against gusty wind,
crack of riverwater slapping against the boat hull,

we careen on ghastly waves through Mutual Gap
into Catastrophe Rapids bending around a village,

and suddenly I long to visit ancients, sage insight-
masters. But I'm old, no idea anymore what to ask.

Traverse Mountain Shrine-Tower

I remember this from fifteen years ago,
this Traverse Mountain shrine. It's still

there at the very summit, tower flashing
radiance onto this crystalline river I sail.

Alone, silent and serene, no incense fire,
it's greeted countless boats. I'm so tired:

how am I facing this shrine-tower again,
bowing to the mountain-Buddha within?

Teasing My Little One

We're stuck on the boat in rain, all cooped up inside.
My little one, the one who's never sad: he's morose,

just sits there, eyes falling closed, then sound asleep.
Finally I suggest bed, and he shakes his head *no, no.*

Waking from a Nap, I Gaze at the Mountain

Rain-squalls on far shores: I can't set out for the summit.
In a dream, I gather bramble-floss and scatter it soaring,

then awake on deck—how marvelous—I see a mountain:
a single fleck of color floating on river wind, cold as ice.

Thinking Through Autumn

2

Done rinsing mouth and face clean, I
settle cap and robe, sit *ch'an* stillness,

then suddenly hold a mirror up to see
myself, and don't recognize who it is.

I've trusted myself, practiced fiercely,
but the years unraveled, and I'm still

not awakened. Gazing at autumn color
or meeting people, I'm blank and sad.

I want to learn from old sage-masters
how they embrace this autumn sorrow,

sorrow of brilliant trees that keeps me
drinking. Wind's unearthly clamor so

full of disappointment, I call for wine,
ladle it out meticulously, languorously,

and soon drunk, don't know who I am,
only what turning seasons make of me.

4

Morning makes autumn's cold bearable,
but I struggle through the endless nights.

Sky-azure lamplight illuminates a book,
but these eyes are soon lost in hazy mist,

so I roll up the scroll and sit by myself,
blockhead, no one anyone could talk to.

I try lying down, but no chance of sleep,
then get up wanting to walk, but where?

Suddenly a corner of the house lights up,
mountain moon come into the courtyard

as if uneasy that I'm alone in origin-dark
night. We gaze all clarity into each other.

I chant, and moon understands perfectly,
then it leaves the gate, and I follow after.

Who needs some old book? Moon and I,
we link lines, make new poems together.

5

My whole life I've hated long summers,
endured them, longed for autumn clarity.

What can I do now that autumn's come
and instead of joy, I'm filled with grief?

I can while away autumn reading books,
exploring poems line by penetrating line,

drink clear through these endless nights,
wander wildland distances far and wide.

Ten thousand rivers and mountains open
through my inch-deep eyes in an instant:

Hey, someone bring those hiking gaiters!
There's a peak to climb everywhere here!

*At No-Reproach Pavilion, Watching a
Spiderweb Under the Eaves*

The spiderweb of openweave grief silently
clings to misty rain. A bug tangles, frantic,

kicking a few drops loose. It's still whole:
this clarity-absolute of ten thousand pearls.

*Passing Gauze-Net Creek, I Look South to the
Wellspring Range*

Wellspring Range peaks all tower up into sharp spires.
Buddha-truth dragons flown off to mountaintops, they

jostle along, studying how I walk. Soon, we share one
journey. It's a kingfisher-green streamer, wind-driven.

At Ten-Mile Lake, Watching Fish

Ten thousand silver ripples weave across the silver lake.
Fish-trap baskets litter the shoreline, where moonlight's

loaded onto fishing boats. Still, the moon itself remains.
What happens when there's no boat, and no moon either?

Cooking Breakfast at Bear-Den Village

It's morning. I'm hungry, but gaze at cook-smoke arcing
along a stream and off into mountains. Here's sight entire

where, hoarding dew in a silk purse, unconcerned with us,
a spider steals bits of smoke, dangles them atop the fence.

Night Landscape at Ten-Mile Lake, Moonlit

Hoping to mirror autumn appearances, I
climb to heights deep in night. Mountain

radiance lights sleeping lakewater; water
reflects it back onto mountain, trembling.

Overnight egrets break into flight, away.
Not gone home: a single fisherman stays.

Old-timer and luminous moon, together
we've opened one harbor of lucid clarity.

Watching Starlings in a Field Pecking at Millet

1

No more bright splendor than crows with their black robes,
and no color, only a white splash half hidden on each wing:

they're so common. Who notices them breaking into flight?
But climbing through sky, they suddenly become blossoms!

2

Millet golden, buckwheat white, and autumn's barely begun.
Who'll recover what those thieves in crow robes have taken,

our public granaries now fluttering around in forest treetops
somewhere? You might find them, but you'd better be quick.

*Passing Below the Traverse Mountain
Shrine-Tower in Autumn*

Between shores, mountains welcome me,
and in these river shallows, willows bow.

Sunlight jostles water cascading through
dragon's whitewater scales. Why not stay?

I'll ask this shrine-tower the way through
our surging and swelling world, and gaze

my whole life at this fluid mirror, seeing
thousands of ages lighting a Buddha face.

The Sound of Pines at a Mountain Inn

In its original-nature, pine is silent. And wind is the same.
But if they happen to meet, they make this sound together,

nothing like chimes and bells, flutes and strings. It's cloud
billowing coast to coast across this vast land of five lakes.

Orchid Creek Shrine-Towers

The tall tower rises into a spire. The short one doesn't.
One sports a brocade robe, and the other a silver tunic.

I ask them why it is they never say a word, but they let
Buddha go on talking in the voice of a tumbling creek.

Reaching Manifest Village

Cragged cliffs towering up, spindled and sinew-thin,
there's no trace of dust, all that human consequence.

Cascading waters wolfed down by a clamoring maw
as if quenching the thirst of some horse running wild,

Catastrophe Rapids pours into Black-Dragon Rapids,
autumn-mountain cliffwalls pinching autumn waters.

It's impossible to ladle out wine's solace on the boat,
so gloom-laden eyes miss dusk's azure-deep purples:

pinnacles in empty skies star-strewn and origin-deep,
floating peaks jade-pure Buddha-terraces, a thousand

wondrous mountains, ten thousand. And then at night
inside courtyard gates, I face a mountain of Absence.

Nightfall, Passing Below Sidelong-Creek Mountain

Facing a wondrous mountain, I see how little I know,
and radiant now in cascades of slant-light, its mystery

deepens: robes full of wrinkles almost cracking open
below peaks rushing distant away, jostling to be first,

and as pine treetops bid six mountains fond farewell,
this mirrored river churns thousands of ranged crags.

Dark confusion floods my wander poems, but here's
Sidelong-Creek: its exact clarities leave nothing out.

Staying Overnight at East Island

2

To see mountains, you need to look within and without.
If you don't, looking at mountains is sheer delusion too.

I'm enthralled all day by ten thousand jade-azure peaks,
at dusk linger out purples on a last few pinnacles. This

wild thusness of mountains all clarity-absolute: no one
sees it. People travel back and forth on riverboats here,

whining about seething whitewater. Pipe down! If you
scare the children, they'll never set out into that clarity.

Wanting to keep this poet's eyes stuffed full, occurrence
worries autumn mountains are too washed-out and dead,

so it unfurls brocade and rouge mist of ancient kingdoms,
billowing lush intricacies across autumn mountain slopes.

Soon, crimson brocade thins into kingfisher-green gauze
as the loom-of-origins weaves out late crows going home,

late crows and kingfisher-green gauze blurring into dark:
nothing to see but a river crystalline as sun-bleached silk.

On the Boat, Sitting at Night

Lush bamboo keeps me from the moon.
Sails can't carry me up into the heavens.

But no sail and no bamboo here, I drift
empty skies star-strewn and origin-deep.

Morning Landscape

River mist, lake fog, village at the edge of darkness.
Everywhere, empty autumn is a single white cloud:

suddenly, these peaks emerge and slowly tower up.
How could mountains this wondrous have no roots?

*My Friend Goes by Boat to Essence-Revere District
on Assignment*

We take a boat from North Gate at dusk, our farewell
lasting as far as Burgeon-Esteem and radiant morning.

Waking from sleep, we find the river full of ice shards,
jewels clittering and clattering together inside a dream.

Late Sun

Infusing river swells, the sun skitters and shatters silvers,
radiant swells frolicking with it, turning it into cold stars.

Suddenly stars fly in boat windows, glint here. Still, vast
transformations of garden and mountain don't even pause.

Autumn, Crossing the Yangtze River

Crystalline frost, icy sky vast, empty: nothing more,
not the least breeze in shoreline plume-grass blooms.

Fog and cloud cleared away, leaving azure distances
east and south. Now, waves mirror sun's radiant reds.

Thousand-year heroes gone beyond swans migrating
away, ancient ruins remain under skies clear of snow.

I carry a waterjar out to the heart of this river's very
mind. Surely water here will make the finest tea ever.

On the Boat, Evening Landscape

Forests of pine stretch along the shoreline ahead. Where
forest trees end, I watch someone out walking. And then

that someone suddenly vanishes behind some mountain.
Announcing a wineshop, jade-azure flags flutter in wind.

Entering Peace-Perpetua Canal Locks

Our boat enters Peace-Perpetua locks in the fifth watch.
What luck: almost home, and here at Overlook-Heights,

dark sky turns to horizon-wide radiance! It's exactly like
nothing else. Silence: barely snow sweeping across sails.

*In the Dream, a Linked Poem of Crimson
and Azure*

Their linked lines teaching such childlike
delight, who could say it's merely dream:

gazing into sky, deep waters glow azure,
and brushing sun, treetops flame crimson?

How could I explain those thoughts, those
minds *ch'i*-deep and impossible to know?

From dark origins comes overnight snow,
then dawn scatters it through empty skies.

***Sent to Be Inscribed on Walls Around
Shadow-Womb Monastery Atop Fierce-
Ease Mountain***

1. Shadow-Womb Monastery

Think of me north of your streams, your
thousand-cliff and ten-thousand-canyon

pavilions. How I envy purple-robe sages
awestruck by even one green-azure peak.

2. Heart-Known Hall

How forlorn the adept's life, traveling
long distances to consult old masters.

If anyone's teaching at Heart-Known,
it's just this autumn-mountain stream.

3. Recluse-Search Hall

I met a sage-elder in dream, face
staring out from my bowl of soup.

Then a silly kid came, fished out
thorn-bean greens, and peered in.

4. Overnight Hut

Here are old masters who can talk all
night without putting anyone to sleep:

open a window onto mountain-moon
liberation, drink to cascading streams.

5. Stone-Gate Crags

Stone confusion heaped into jade-pure
crags makes paired peaks an easy gate:

feet soiled by this world's dust never
walk among eddying gate-crag clouds.

6. Sight-Perfected Meditation Hall

Autumn trying to see the world whole?
Stone trying to see it hewn into things?

To understand Ch'an's deep hard-won
realization, simply give them both up.

7. Cold-Tower Inn

Mist thickened into warm robes—dew-
lit, jade-white. Dawn's thusness-clarity.

Past midnight, a lone crane was calling:
feathered person in moonlight returning.

8. Sunset-View Pavilion

Alone in cities, great recluses can face
kingfisher-green paintings, where sun-

set never ends. Who cares? You can so
easily climb to this pavilion and watch.

9. *Iron-Flute Pavilion*

Who can make black-lacquer metal
chant with a bamboo flute's clarity?

Beyond forests, a single note: rock
thundering down a thousand peaks.

10. *Fishhook Jetty*

Come drunk in moonlit night, dangle
bent hook into this Nine-Bend River.

In water this clear, not a fish in sight,
fishhooks are crescent moons of jade.

11. *Tea-Stove Peak*

Tea-Stove began as a peaked rainhat
worn by a farmer in the tea kingdom:

it flew here to Fierce-Ease Mountain.
The creek's mind has turned to stone.

12. *Fishing Boat*

How could this monastery be far away?
It's here on Nine-Bend River. You can

come by boat. Stay home, and it seems
like Star River ten thousand miles away.

Evening Cold: Narcissus Among Lakes and Mountains

1

Full of warm dharma, narcissus love cold clarity.
I sleep lazily for two toasty days. Tonight, bitter-

cold evening winds. No people. Only narcissus:
lit mountain-Buddhas for company in this poem.

2

There's no wind. Still, the lake's face is ice-cold.
Closing our boat's cabin door, I open the insight

gateway: I don't see my three toppled winecups
as if mountains dotting some lakeshore expanse.

Refine lines, forge poems: how could poems
encompass Absence, how could they exhaust

origin-tissue itself? This old-timer doesn't go
hunting for poems, they come hunting for me.

Reading the Ancients

Too hot in the sun, and bothered by hornets, I try
cool shade on the terrace. Pestered by mosquitos,

I return to sun. Nowhere lit clarity or dark-enigma
depths. Hornet hind-legs jointed yellow and black.

At All-Water Altars, Gazing Across the South Lake Landscape in Evening Light

1

I watch fishing lanterns amid South Lake waters,
geese landing, wakes near shoreline silver-grass.

Seen as depths, two peaks tower into rainy mist.
As appearance, they burgeon all inception itself.

3

South wind blasts in like an onslaught of arrows,
then a sedge-weave sail flies up the tallest mast.

Suddenly, willows along both shores are running
alongside. And yet, they stay just where they are.

Crossing Open-Anew Lake

1

How marvelous: ten thousand miles of jade-azure
water, gauze-weave ripples crystalline to far edges,

or stretching south all the way into sky. Then more
perfect still: weave dissolved into glassy distances.

2

A fisherman's taking his boat deep across the lake.
My old eyes trace his path all the way, his precise

wavering in and out of view. Then it gets strange:
suddenly, he's a lone goose balanced on bent reed.

7. Dwell-Deep Studio

This breath-space seed-time Cosmos is our
lone wayhouse. Who's the innkeeper, empty-

mind host gone free and far away? It's okay:
there's still firewood stacked near the stove.

9. Mountain Studio

Old masters spent their nights in this studio,
and kindred-spirit guests never stopped by.

When this radiant moon didn't come, those
white-cloud minds had no one for company.

10. *Drunken Rock*

Ladling out wine at night, then easily drunk,
I lose track of what's me and what darkness.

How wondrous! Sprawled amid black-azure
fields, I doze until dear moon comes to visit.

13. *Bamboo Studio*

It's bitter bitter cold, season of frost and ice,
time to cultivate a mind of jade-white snow.

Sage poems and sutras teach nothing of this.
They can't voice moon's mind-transmission.

14. *Ancient-Three Pavilion*

Two trees here possessing long-ago beauty,
calm and composed, not like today's world:

they say the ancients are gone, but in these
moonlit nights, I hear shoes scuffing on air.

23. *White-Crane Pavilion*

How tender, lone crane in these gardens:
it's a friend willing to keep me company,

while longing to soar across the heavens.
Listen—it keeps calling out to the moon.

33. *Gone-Cold Pavilion*

Cold, laughing, I taste dark-enigma Absence,
then alone at this height, I'm done with mind.

Eyes adoring orchard blossoms: who can use
those eyes to see through this world of snow?

35. *Ginkgo Crag*

Called *white*, confetti isn't white absolute.
Labeled *red*, banners are nothing like red.

Try this: done with festive red and white,
eyes renewed, gaze into occurrence itself.

36. *Peony Hedge*

At sunrise, peonies flaunt such elegant beauty,
and in wind, wood-irises offer their wild scents.

Meditation cushions, Buddha-nature talismans:
come outside for a way free of all that wisdom.

50. *Radiance All-Gaze Monastery*

Forest of slant-light ablaze deep in the eye,
chill of setting moon drifting wide on wind,

I settle into rivers and mountains. Together,
we're a single distance of autumn radiance.

*Wandering Up to Bell Mountain's Samadhi-Forest
Monastery and the Library of Thorn-Bramble Master
Wang An-shih*

Bell Mountain stands deep among ten thousand mountains.
Come into these very depths again, I enter Samadhi-Forest,

all the way in, to clarities of rock and pine. Then I keep on
further still, to the sage shrine-hut: peak amid white clouds.

Midday Drowse

Eyes drooping. Wild tumbledown hair. A long drowsy day:
I toss a book of poems aside, wander around the courtyard.

The cats are out, frolicking happily together here and there.
Suddenly, seeing some person arrive, they scatter like deer.

Moon Terrace, Sitting at Night

1

Autumn days continue blistering hot,
but nights are such crystalline clarity.

I keep coming back, old man sitting
amid frost deep into this third watch:

stars in fitful wind flare and go dark,
moon hosts clouds traveling through.

Heron-wild joy: to seek it is to lose it,
but tonight, out of nowhere, here it is!

2

Sunset is, for a moment, pure answer.
Stars begin to appear, brilliant. They

assemble like jade-white chess pieces
crowding the black-azure board, then

suddenly rain moves in, a downpour.
Later into the night, skies clear again.

Cricket voices mingle with mine. This
autumn lament: at bottom, whose is it?

On the Market Road in Manifest-Vast, Cooking
Breakfast Beside a Painted Bridge

Gossamer-thin mist edges into empty autumn sky.
High amid pine treetops, a million sparkles gather.

Soon they've swollen into large drops falling and
all around, suddenly on open umbrellas, clattering.

Bubbles on Water

Faint sun, sparse clouds: scattered raindrops send
bubbles skipping and skittering across crystalline

ditch water. Here in each drop, I find the Buddha-
truth pearl black-dragon guards in its riverbed lair.

At Farewell Cove

The ox path I'm on ends in a rabbit trail, and suddenly
I'm facing open plains and empty sky on all four sides.

My thoughts follow white egrets—a pair taking flight,
leading sight to a million green-azure mountains rising

ridge beyond ridge, my gaze lingering out near and far,
enthralled by peaks crowded together or drifting alone.

Even a hill or valley means thoughts beyond knowing—
and all this? A crusty old man's now a wide-eyed child!

Torches Ablaze Outside the Inn at Oath-Token Ferry

1

Ashes swirling up into empty skies settle as dawn stars,
then carried on wind across fields, they become autumn

fireflies. It confuses water-crickets. They think morning
light's back, shift their song from cold rhythms to warm.

2

Yesterday noon on my meditation cushion, autumn light
flared! But this morning, I'm in no hurry for radiant sun.

Flax-twig cooking fire illuminates three thousand miles:
it's a blazing torch of golden lotus blossom come to life.

*Reach the City and Reward-Heavens Monastery
in the Fifth Watch, Then Go at First Light to Meet
the Master*

Along the stream, dawn frost lines both banks.
At the bridge, a hundred boats in autumn wind.

I threaded through narrow streets, then set out,
and soon, I'm gazing down at city walls far off.

Drifting low, the moon makes a perfect friend,
and a faint bell seems to announce the meeting.

I pause at a pavilion halfway up this mountain,
change horses, then go to face the craggy peak.

Appearance Itself

Setting, bathing in clear-sky river, mountain sun
veins its single radiance out along clear streams.

A thousand peaks gather all four distances close.
A lone city seethes up dead-center in riverwater.

Terraced shrine-towers jade-white among clouds.
Autumn willows mirrored on shorelines. Pilgrim

leaving a lofty pavilion to exhaust depths of sight,
I climb this mountain into horizon-wide clarities.

*On Our Boat Near the Vast-Fathom
City Markets*

River clouds billow up to cliffwalls.
Lashing waves slap at frontier skies.

We've given up on wind filling sails:
it's in our face, churning wild water,

and fishermen keep their silver-grass
nets cast wide, blocking our passage.

Why complain to the river goddess?
For her, crab and fish have no price.

*Cooking Breakfast in Morning Dark at Renew-Forest, I
Watch Bell Mountain Appear*

I said farewell and left Bell Mountain behind a month ago,
and now, how could it recognize me returning north again?

It doesn't even know my name; and yet, how tenderhearted,
suddenly drawing near here outside this country wayhouse.

*1st Moon, 4th Sun, Water Year of the Rat: Wandering
the Back Garden After Misty Rain*

Facing sage teachings spring radiance offers, I'm lucky
wine's at hand, though I'm old, and its depths scare me.

Sunlight splendor hidden within earth's colors: I find it
here in this web shuddering as a spider scurries across.

Awake, Can't Sleep

Barely drunk, though I had plenty,
this cold night seems to last years.

Awakened, I wrote out my dream,
but then couldn't get back to sleep,

ten thousand worries settling here
before my eyes. By the third watch,

grief clear and out of control: it's
a goose crying across frosty skies.

Passing the Night at Recluse-Roost Monastery in This City, I Gaze Again at Traverse Mountain

Seeing Traverse Mountain renews my watery old eyes:
it's a mountain monk saying *Get free of your public self.*

Dragon-lanterns, pipes and drums: every year another
spring festival, crowds and wine, orioles and blossoms:

suddenly, I remember long-ago peony-sangha masters,
and turning, face five oaks I knew one long-ago spring.

Outland cloud, wildland moon. Monastery abandoned,
empty: for sleeves, I have wind; for a cap, blown dust.

Arriving to Stay Overnight at Devotion-Sage Ch'an Monastery on White-Cloud Mountain

The path narrows, greens of ancient pines lighting earth,
then I see a tower spiring into clouds. Leaving the forest,

I see rooflines, realize I've nearly reached the monastery,
blossoms so thick I can't see singing orioles. And higher,

I gaze out across White-Cloud to a thousand more peaks,
and down to a lone stream cascading along slopes below.

Mountain cold pierces my bones. They feel like ice now,
and soon monks join me, speaking the very clarity of ice.

On Thousand-Buddha Tower at Devotion-Sage Monastery

In the eye, one peak is wild wonder. Seen one by one,
each peak is again wild wonder. If I love a mountain,

I talk like no other compares. But if I can keep quiet,
millions of green-azure peaks rise ridge beyond ridge.

Staying Overnight at Three-Mile Inn, I'm Kept Awake All Night by the Racket of Cascading Streamwater

Tumbledown post-station, overgrown village: here
on a mountain road, crosswinds and fine rain, I sit

facing my lamp. All night, a cuckoo calls and calls.
That stream's racket must be keeping it awake too.

On the Summit Above Tranquil-Joy Monastery

Who says poets are so enthralled with mountains? Mountains,
mountains, mountains—I've raved on and on, and they're still

clamoring for attention. A thousand peaks, ten thousand ridges:
it's too much for me. If I climb an hour, I need to rest for three.

When your desk is piled full, you just can't add anything more,
and when your withered stomach is full, who can keep eating?

So what good's even a faint scrap of mist or kingfisher-green?
I'll wrap it all up, send the whole bundle off to my city friends.

Climbing Out of Forests Below Tranquil-Joy Monastery,
I Gaze at the Frost-Chime Range, Its Two High Peaks
Perfectly Wild with Eerie Wonder

Old masters detest mountains, stay clear of them. Alone
at the empty center of things, they gaze into the Buddha-

nature jewel. Here, forests ribbon over the lower slopes,
and two peaks poke up out of cloud like bamboo-shoots,

glimpsed for a moment, then vanishing into cloud again,
piercing my bones with the perfect freeze of their eerie

clarities. Distinctions given up, we inhabit origin-tissue
dharma. So why mangle lofty peaks with hate and love?

Ox-Herding at Tranquil-Joy Monastery

First comes the child tugging an ox across streamwater,
and then, riding an ox, another turns to ask something.

Tucking flowers into a straw rainhat, a third plays flute,
and yet another is carried by mama ox leading her calf.

Spring streamwater delicate and clear, no trace of mire,
spring grasses along the island gossamer and jade-pure,

five oxen wander off, far off—no one controlling them.
And that village across the stream: it's where all these

kids live. Some raindrops hit a bare head, and suddenly
three rainhats and four thatch raincloaks scamper home.

On Peace-Renew River at Sunrise, I Gaze at Purple-Brights Mountain and Think of My Friend, Dark-Moon Origin

My old friend long ago lived below Purple-Brights Mountain,
but now he's somewhere amid House-Snake Mountain peaks,

a recluse gone back home, no more wandering. And I'm here
like some divination master, reading our future in river winds.

At Peak-Soar Ferry, Setting Out into Flat Country

Streams vein ten thousand mountains above mountains,
then here, half a moon drifts river-flooded sky in fields.

Out beyond the fields, vast sky draws near, touches this
river's mind: a single eye limitless in all four directions.

Spring Mountains in Rain

Who conjured spring mountains anew?
Beyond a veil of pinnacles spiring up

into skies painted pale, just raw paper.
Flecks of light stitch across mountains,

mountains and mountains far beyond,
three thousand miles traced on paper.

Dusky mountain distances thin lonely
grief, ancient summit pines jade-azure,

pines towering each higher into cloud,
windblown jade-azures lit deeper still.

Dusty pigment sprinkled and brushed
lightly thins in a moment, transparent

pines opening jade-azure into nothing,
distant mountains barely half sketched.

Morning, I Set Out from Dharma-Awakening Monastery
and Follow a Stream Up Through Impossible
Crags and Distances Toward a Mountain Pass

Rivers and mountains and no bridges or village smoke,
boundless flood of streamwater racket and hissing rain.

Two egrets warmly offer good cheer. But it's hopeless:
I soon leave them for nirvana-still desolation on and on.

In a Bamboo-Weave Skiff, Gazing at the Moon

I moor my boat to an old willow in spring. Clouds
clear: a thousand peaks, a river flooded with moon-

light. Leaping to shore, I enter a cold moon-palace:
looking down into jade-azure mirror, I see only sky,

and suddenly, ten thousand stars turn to snowflakes,
then I'm awake long ago, a city's third watch, gone

home again. O, telling dream in the midst of dream
like this, I take flight free of all cause or condition.

On a Boat, Crossing Through Peace-Humane District

2

Distant mountains appear, like a painting, and I'm in love,
then suddenly they're furled away, blank as Absence itself.

They can't fool this old-timer, sight still bright with clarity:
even in those depths of mist and cloud, they're open to me.

3

Out on the merest wisp of a fishing boat, two small boys
give up the struggle. They ship their paddles and just sit.

It seems so strange. No rain in sight, they start opening
umbrellas. Not for shelter. They want to sail on the wind!

Desolation Chants

*Facing headwinds, we anchor for three days in the midst
of this empty-mind lake, off a small island beside Ease-
Master Mountain.*

1

After a life on mountain roads, I can't bear more mountains,
and now crossing this lake, I'm stopped dead by headwinds.

I've wandered this world, boats and carriages, never settled.
Boundless heaven and earth: maybe that's all I am anymore.

3

Buffeting night, wind turns heaven and earth topsy-turvy,
churns up lakewater, heaves it through the edge of heaven.

Ease-Master floating up free of its vanished roots, I moor
my boat to an island drifting vast Northern-Dipper depths.

5

Books just annoy me. I can't bear to read them anymore.
And poetry bores me to death. I'm sick of all its insight.

But my vagabond mind is restless, never at ease and still:
guess I'll count the raindrops trickling down this window.

7

Done chanting new poems, I feel tired. Soon, I'm asleep,
a lazy butterfly floating clear through the eight distances.

Outside the boat, wind and waves crash like wild thunder,
but it's perfectly silent here in this land of sleep: sky, sky.

8

How is there cook-smoke here amid this lake's empty-mind,
skies mirrored above and below, and two flecks of mountain?

Four boats tied together, dogs barking and roosters crowing:
in this vast kingdom of water wheeling around, it's a village!

9

Here on the boat, we only have food for today. And out here
on this lake's empty-mind expanse, there's no village market.

To live forever, ascetics stop eating. But how do I learn their
mysterious methods by tomorrow, when breakfast is nothing?

Wind tipping sky up, crashing waves against mountaintops:
there's nothing to do but laugh. What good is worried grief?

Two days here stretch into three. It's a blessing, exhaustion
absolute: I've found the tranquil depths of giving myself up.

Sailing the River Past Blaze-Array Mountains, I Gaze Far Off to Succession-Brights Mountain

Heaven-Ferry stars harbor moon, wheel around my dreams.
Then we sail from Tenderheart Lake, and I break into smile.

Nearby peaks filling my eye: we recognize each other whole.
And in sight's emptiest clarity, that far peak is *samadhi*-still.

As Our Boat Passes the Swan-Chant River's Mouth, Chicken-Basket Peak Fills My Gazing Eyes

It's been two unrelenting months of jade-azure mountains,
and soon in the city, it will seem I never knew mountains.

Ten thousand peaks come to bid farewell, then drift away.
Only Chicken-Basket stays with me: it can't bear leaving.

III

LATE POEMS

(1192–1206: Age 65–79)

1st Moon, Water Year of the Ox: I Open the Old East Garden Anew, Clear Its Nine Paths

I always hated being too poor to build gardens, but returning home again, I discover the east garden still here, still lovely.

I clear *samadhi*-serene paths, then only one worry remains: I can't afford all those sandals I'll wear out wandering here.

Nine Paths Samadhi-*Serene*

> *I've opened my east garden's paths anew. Three times three, nine of them crowded with river-plum and sea-apple, peach and summer-plum, tangerine and apricot, winter-plum, jade-peach, showy rose-mallow: nine types of flowering trees, one for each path. Three-deep three-shadowed earth: I call them my nine paths samadhi-serene.*

Opening three paths made this Wang An-shih's recluse home. The second three made me another T'ao Ch'ien.

And now, I myself have nine lavish paths all *samadhi*-serene. For me, the path in bloom is the path I wander.

***After Snow, Winter-Plums in Bloom, I Look Around My
East Garden at Midday***

Where skies hint at opening, it's the color of pale shadow.
I'm sober again after a midday nap, my mind clear. Light

snow: still, a plum branch broke, crashed onto the house.
Clouds clear, and East Mountain's high peak breaks free.

All wind and light, original-nature can't comfort old age,
and how can sage insight answer these ravages of winter?

Lunch is lamb's-ear and baby-greens, fledge-wine. Then
drunk again, I enter the plum grove and turn into a wasp.

*Early Autumn, Keeping Cool on the Stone Terrace
Beside My Pond and Its Lotus Blossoms*

A lotus petal tumbles down and becomes a boat. Breezes
ruffle it, stuck there against a towering parasol-leaf stalk.

It sticks, then drifts on; drifts, then sticks again. I watch:
it's roaming everywhere all through this water-deep sky.

Visiting a Friend in the City, the Night Hot, I Can't Sleep

Heat venomous all night, sleep unimaginable, I get up
and wander along the pool this house faces. Suddenly

a star streaks way down into these silver-bowl depths,
turns the whole crystalline mirror of sky upside down.

*On the Second Day After the 9/9 Festival, Manifest-Able
and I Climb Up into Ten-Thousand-Blossom Canyon,
Where We Share a Cup of Wine Beside the River*

My old-timer thirst is desperate, but moon's even worse.
When a little wine tumbles into my cup, moon's already

there, shepherding heaven's azure expanse deep inside,
both of them, heaven and moon, utterly stewed in wine,

so if the ancients deny *heaven treasures wine*, and claim
moon has never understood wine—I know it's nonsense.

I lift my winecup and swill moon down in a single gulp,
then look up to discover moon still there in the heavens:

that's when my bottomless old-timer laugh begins and I
ask my friend: *Is moon itself a single sphere, or is it two?*

Once wine gets into a poem's gut, wind and fire swell up,
and once moon gets in, there's ice and snow everywhere,

then before a single cup's drunk dry, the poem's finished,
me chanting it out, startling heaven itself. And how do I

know all boundless history's a scatter of bleached bones?
I just ladle out a fresh cup and swill down another moon.

*Sent to Be Inscribed on Walls Around Blade-
Moon's House*

2. Gossamer-Haze Studio

Empty as Northern Dipper depths, mind abides
like the ten thousand transformations *samadhi-*

still. Or like gossamer haze spread across this
dark abyss. Why not paint a bright face there?!

5. Winejar Sky

It's large enough to fill earth's nine distances,
and small enough to abide in a single winejar.

Gaze tranquil into that sky of original-nature
here, large and small together: what can it be?

*Written on a Wall at Snow-Chill Monastery, Where
Whitewater Rapids Pause in the Dark-Enigma Pools*

Out of the west a thousand miles and more, Early-Treasure
River comes cascading, fierce as a tiger, its whiskers pulled.

Here, banners stream out over rooftops like flashing swords,
water tumbling like the Yangtze itself, shouting *KHO-AAA!*,

seething and churning where Snow Mountain is utterly still,
splashing everywhere, scattering spray to a meditation-hall.

Guests gaze at waves blasting into peach-blossom sprinkles,
but I can't see this ice-wild water clear through, every wave

crashing against mind's empty window fearless against cold.

On a Spring Day, Wood Year of the Hare, I Stroll in
Idleness Among My Three Paths

I wander this east garden all day, a thousand turns around,
watching dragon take flight again, spring beginning anew:

peach and plum spreading leaves, and me far into old age,
rivers and mountains ancient, but fresh yet again this year.

I peer into blossoms, roam textures and forms: all day this
instant of pure confusion. I hear voices, but no one's there.

Search out old companions? They're all scattered as stars.
And white clouds drifting mountains make perfect friends.

Sent to Pilgrim-Monk Idle-Cloud on Black-Hut Mountain

A flake of cloud unfurls off Black-Hut Peak and comes
transformed into this pilgrim-monk visiting at my gate.

I ask about an idle cloud's wild thusness-clarity insight:
Just drift on the wind village to village, anywhere at all.

Eating Frost to Sober Up

Wine all night, and come morning I'm still plastered:
stuffed with fuzz, ears ringing, stomach a fiery mess.

On these peony garden steps, stone below the railing,
I scrape frost into a ball, roll it around on my tongue.

*My Inkstone's Water-Bowl Full of Wine, Winter-Plum
and Chrysanthemum Blossoms Fall In, One Each*

Two branches of late chrysanthemum, two of early plum:
blossoms fall into my bowl of jade wine. Thirsty for wild

thusness-clarity, I harbor high hopes for this pool of joy:
chrysanthemum, plum, ripe wine—that makes three cups.

Rain Dripping Off Eaves

Rain dripping off eaves: how much clarity can it reveal?
It tumbles into a round basin, spills sheer insight across

moss-lit terrace stones, scours them clean. And beyond,
it doesn't muddy anything. There's a nice bed of gravel.

In the Small Pond, Rain Clatters on Waterlily Leaves

Dozing at noon, I dream of drifting on misty West Lake
long ago, guiding the boat in among waterlily blossoms,

when a quick rain-clatter drums on the jumble of leaves,
startling me awake to wild tumbledown hair, aging eyes.

It's rain bouncing and skittering all over my waterlilies,
exquisite pearls of thusness-clarity. They scatter further

and gather back; flurry, turning water silver; then finally
spill off leaves into clearing water, nowhere to be found.

Spring Night, No Sleep, Thoughts a Tangled Confusion of Worry

175

I can't bear this world's ten thousand worries tearing me apart,
walling me in. I break free into the open country wine reveals,

and when wine's magic fades, I keep moving. The brief spring
night ends, and I continue on further and further. My thoughts

and despairs floating all idleness, scattering numberless away:
seed-fluff drifting out through all eight directions. This world

lit at the east window: suddenly, a single dream stretches clear
back to first-emperor Root-Breath—half human, half dragon.

Autumn Begins, a Little Rain, but Summer's
Fierce Heat Doesn't Ease

What marvelous rain! But why so little?
It hardly brings a hint of cool freshness,

and when gusts howling across roof-tiles
end, even these waterlilies are dry again.

Dragons are so very like us, aren't they?
Don't they too hate this heat, fling river-

lightning into sky? I'll just ask them to
drag Star River's chill down among us.

An old adage says lightning-flashes are
dragons flinging riverwater into the sky.

Inscribed on Occurrence-Lavish Tower

1

Old-timer topsy-turvy wild on wine, I inscribe sincere poems
on towers and walls, rocks and cliffs. It's serene, a deep bow,

but why would these mountains read such emaciated words?
Moon and cloud scrawl out their pageant, and it's all a poem.

2

On this tower, incense of azure-weave sky infuses my bones,
and radiance of jade-green peaks lights empty-mind stillness.

Now, I can soar on wind up into the temple of cold expanses
where autumn cloud is a single fleck of silvered-azure below.

Sent to Be Inscribed on Kingfisher-Flood Tower

South of the library terrace, mountains surrounding rooftops
look like ten thousand hairpins of sharpened sky-azure jade,

and north of the library terrace, even more mountains spread
like a blue sea of ten thousand leaping and billowing waves.

Here beside the terrace, our lofty friend Master Blade-Moon
built a tower in the midst of these mountains north and south,

and today, deep in drunkenness, we follow him up to the top.
Suddenly, earth's a startling drift of kingfisher-green waves,

waves heaving froth and cloud halfway up through heaven,
churning empty sky upside down, flooding Star River itself,

as shattering thunder comes tumbling over the tower railing,
land and sky seething, *yang*-deep heaven and *yin*-deep earth

all topsy-turvy. We clap and call for a boat, ready to set sail,
but by the time we can see straight, none of all that remains:

it's just countless flecks of peak stretching everywhere away.

Why travel harvest-yellow mountain valleys,
and why speak of rock-root tangerine groves?

Here, this isolate cliffwall spires into pinnacle,
casts shadow into the vast river's very mind,

and I can hear these voices of autumn insects
like monks chanting insight through the night.

Hermit-plums make me long for the ancients.
Otherwise, I just settle into origin-dark quiet.

Summer Night, at Play with the Moon

I look up: moon's there in heaven
casting my shadow onto the earth.

When I walk, shadow also walks,
and when I pause, shadow pauses,

so I can't fathom shadow and me:
are we simply one, or are we two?

Only moon can paint this shadow.
If I try alone, it's no shadow at all,

so I come wandering at this stream,
moon alight in streamwater. Here,

moon numbers two, high and low,
as if each were the true full moon,

or is it that streamwater is heaven,
or maybe heaven this streamwater?

Autumn, Up Early

A rooster calls out, but not the bell.
No idea how close dawn may be, I

get up, but afraid I'll startle others,
don't dare open windows or doors.

A night lamp sputters low, radiance
shining like broom-brush into dark.

I look closer, closer. Suddenly, it's
lightning flashing into flight away.

Night, I Sip Wine

Night, I sip wine in my studio's cold
emptiness, wander back to the stove.

This fresh wine ripened just in time,
and last night's candle-ends remain,

purple fiddleheads bigger than fists,
gold tangerines sweeter than honey.

Once I'm drunk, poems come to me:
I grab a brush, find nothing to write.

Sleeplessness

After the full moon, nights deepened toward this moonless
dark. Crickets hide beneath thick frost. It's perfectly silent.

All idleness and joy in itself, my mind is clear streamwater
conjuring even out of sleeplessness ten thousand thoughts.

Drying My Clothes

At noon, I hang clothes out to dry. Later, I fold them
into a willow and plaincloth basket, carry them inside.

My wife and daughter both laugh and ask each other:
Look at that old guy: bare feet, white hair! Who is he?

1st Moon, 7th Sun, Water Year of the Dog, Birthday of Humankind Born of Dragons: A Spring Day at South Creek

I sit here watching white cloud appear amid blue skies,
then form into a baby dragon, scales of silver cymbals.

Pretty soon, it's grown huge, blotting out all that blue,
and I only see dragon scales. I can't see its body at all.

Sent to Be Written on Cloud-Blown Mountain Tower

I often imagine Li Po's billowy robes. Today,
I raise these blinds, and my eyes go ice-cold:

a thousand ridges billowing cloud above blue
ridges come soaring inside and dance, dance.

Wandering Countryside Colors

This drop holds the jade-blue of every stream,
that blossom reveals springtime in mountains.

Fields of young rice bask in the early warmth,
and amid thatch huts, signs of repair are fresh.

Cold Chickens

Cold chickens sleep on. They don't care if it's morning,
or if some bell bangs, waking us people to another day.

Tomorrow, I'll ignore the dawn bell and go on sleeping.
The others laugh at chickens: why would they scold me?

Celebrating the Autumn Festival, I Go Wandering at
Cloud-Frontier Monastery

Golden towers and profound library, kingfisher-green peaks:
the bell's call carries down slopes where white clouds begin.

This person who roamed eastern rivers, and this South Creek:
how can I understand myself? I come asking sage mountains,

and they dye my robes with ridgeline blues and lake greens,
stain my cold skin with gossamer blossom and scented mist.

They'll see thousands more autumn festivals, and I ask them,
then wander tasting dark-enigma origin, companion to egrets.

After Winter Solstice, Traveling to the City

Between solstice and midwinter festivals, bitter tangles of
plum blossom yet to come, butterflies return to warm days.

Sunlight across distant forest lights up this lake, trembles,
shatters water, then tips mountain reflections upside-down.

Noon Sun

I put up a drying rack, lay my robes out in sun to dry.
It's the hour for visits, but I turn away to sun my back.

Spring began in last night's snow, and no one noticed,
but out starting new webs, spiders already understand.

Evening Walk Among Fields

1

Cuckoos calling, sun's cloud-streak flare sinks away.
My gaunt walking-stick wants to set out, look around

western fields: pearls of dew climb young rice leaves
partway and stop—no need to ignite sleek green tips.

2

These level fields are flooded end to end with water,
a single sheet of cloud-stained paper spreading away

in rain. Rice-starts planted haphazard look like words:
who says mountain farmers can't understand writing?

12th Moon, 27th Sun, Season Spring Begins: A Night Without Sleep

Resenting endless winter nights, I was longing for spring, and now spring nights are worse. So what is there to say?

I scrunch my eyes closed, but it doesn't help. I can't sleep. I rub the soles of my feet together, but they're no warmer.

And all night there's wind among pines. I listen til dawn, watching a lamp's clear light smolder darker and darker:

suddenly I sit up, grab the quilt and pull it over my head, then realize it's me casting that shadow of a sick monkey.

Sick, Feet Hurting Again, I Sit Exhausted All Day:
A Poem to Ease My Grief

Blossoming shadow fills my eyes, and snow my hair.
It's been like this three or four years. And today, how

could people know I don't walk because of sick feet?
Everyone thinks I'm meditating here, inhabiting Way.

If I drop my fan at the desk, I'm too lazy to pick it up,
and I can't read books beneath that window anymore.

People long to join the immortals and just soar away;
I long to walk like people: they're the real immortals.

Morning After Rain, I Wake and Go Out
to Look at Mountains

Waking, I go out my bramblewood gate,
and peaks across lakewater confuse me.

Looking closely, I see they're the same,
but the color is different than yesterday:

it's true we had rain last night, but how
could rain change them this completely?

Sage-master clouds floated these peaks
there in the middle of indigo-jade water:

silk-green adrift above shoreline fields,
leek-green added above grassland trees,

autumn's rack and ruin has begun again,
so how can mountains look like spring?

All of this means something, something
deep enough to captivate this old-timer:

it seems the incisive clarity of our quick
words could explain, but they never can,

and even if they could, they say nothing
like the depths in all this mountain color.

7th Moon, 7th Sun: Sick

What luck, this exquisite landscape: I can't stay away.
Here, bitter grief crowding my thoughts is a mountain

where cicada song crosses a stream to charm willows,
and blossoms scatter yellow snow among scholar-trees.

Amid so much sickness, mind itself can't be beautiful,
but it's early autumn, and I'm all *adoration* facing this

windblown world. I talk kid-talk now, seek no insight:
the simpler this old-timer gets, the craftier he becomes.

7th Moon, 8th Night: I Sit Meditating in Moonlit Dew

193

Summer-blaze clouds thinning to turmeric-heat clouds,
I take cushions out past eaves and settle my sick body

at the ancient well, draw fresh water among cliffwalls.
Moss, terrace-stone, island blossoms: no floating dust

here, only clear skies. Wind rustles, and then goes still.
And not at all cool itself, how could bamboo cool me?

But soon, I know only tonight's crescent moon, rising,
drifting treetops, sifting down dew: my new gauze cap.

Self-Portrait

Clear wind demands chanted poems,
and radiant moonlight requires wine.

Drunk, I tumble flat amid blossoms,
heaven my blanket, earth my pillow.

Getting Free

Why make this sickness into such heart-scorching grief?
As mountain, I'll still wander; as stone, I'll sleep deeply.

And for now, I'm just like sick wind, the same sick feet.
Old, old man—I must be some immortal roaming earth.

After Rain Clears, I See Peach and Plum Blooming in the East Garden, So I Wander Along the Stream, Wanting to See Deep into Things Themselves

Medicine's my gateway to mind, settles my churning heart,
and to drive away isolate desolation, I go to the east garden,

walk deeply into its nine *samadhi*-serene paths one by one,
wander here and there through blossoming reds and whites.

I look into deep-shadow trees, and see no murky confusion,
watch streamwater tumbling past, and find no grief-tangles.

I roam village after village of peach and plum, and beyond,
until my feet ache bitterly. Then I sit gazing into mountains.

Sick, Studying a Mirror

1

Waking sick, my bones are old all over
again. Easy things aren't easy anymore.

My vision is ringed around with jewels,
my waist thin as a blossom-lost wasp's,

and facing myself, I recognize nothing.
Who is this I'm suddenly meeting here?

Nothing remaining now of that person I
am: what further depths could I fathom?

2

Studying a mirror, I suddenly wonder
where this old-timer is, alone and sick.

Outside town on the far shores of life,
deep in the open country wine reveals,

he leaves inkstone and brush deserted,
wine jar and cup day after day empty.

Touching his snow-flecked hair, time-
etched, I turn and gaze into west wind.

Reading Ancient Poems at Night

In this recluse life all origin-dark quiet,
I'm content. Why make clarity of grief?

Two scrolls and two windows, and each
poem I chant brings another tear. Moon

deep in the third watch: it alone knows
my mind of ten thousand lost ages gone.

Sickness drifts back. Wine's forbidden.
I stop chanting poems. Then start again.

NOTES

To avoid disrupting the direct experience of the poems, notes are not indicated in the poems themselves. Instead, the notes below are simply keyed to page numbers.

Yang Wan-li's poems assume the Taoist/Ch'an conceptual framework shared by all artist-intellectuals of ancient China. That framework is made up of a constellation of key philosophical concepts, concepts that appear in the poems without explanation. These concepts are explained in the Key Terms section (p. 209 ff.). That section can be read piecemeal, as the concepts are encountered in the poems (notes at the first occurrence of each term reference the Key Terms section), or it can be read whole as an introduction to Taoist/Ch'an understanding. That understanding is described more completely in my *China Root: Taoism, Ch'an, and Original Zen*.

There is one other English translation of Yang Wan-li's poems: Jonathan Chaves's *Heaven My Blanket, Earth My Pillow* (1975). J. D. Schmidt's scholarly introduction to Yang is *Yang Wan-li* (1976).

4 **Winter-Plum:** In Yang Wan-li's southern China, there were varieties of plum that bloomed in winter: a frequent image in Yang's poems.

   origin-dark quiet: See Key Terms, p. 210.

5 **year's-end:** A time of year that recurs often in Yang Wan-li's poems. In the Chinese calendar, the New Year corresponds to

the beginning of spring, coming sometime between late January and late February. And so, year's-end is perhaps late January: late winter, with spring imminent.

Tu Fu: T'ang Dynasty poet (712–760 C.E.) who lived four centuries before Yang Wan-li. See my *The Selected Poems of Tu Fu: Expanded and Newly Translated*.

6   **eyelids peeled away . . . :** Ch'an enlightenment is sometimes described as eyelids peeled away, leaving awakened sight wide-open.

    wine: See Key Terms, p. 214.

11   **idleness:** See Key Terms, p. 213.

12   **grand and wondrous . . . affair:** Ch'an term for this whole marvelous world of transformation.

17   This poem is thinking back to these lines in T'ao Ch'ien's famous "Drinking Wine" (#5):

> Picking chrysanthemums
> at my east fence, I see South Mountain
>
> far off: air lovely at dusk, birds in flight
> going home. All this means something,
>
> some thusness-clarity itself absolute:
> to explain it, I forget words altogether.

The connection appears in the concept of 真, translated here as "thusness-clarity itself absolute," and referenced in the poem's "thusness." This concept is central to the Taoist/Ch'an tradition, and is explained more fully in the Key Terms (*Thusness*), p. 212.

19   *prajna:* A state of perfect wisdom in which mind is returned to its original-nature. See Key Terms, p. 214.

20   **Absence:** See Key Terms, p. 209.

21   **wild thusness . . . clarity-absolute:** See Key Terms, p. 212.

24   One of the few poems Yang Wan-li wrote in the *tz'u* form. *Tz'u* are modeled after song lyrics, and have a more relaxed and spontaneous feel, reflected in their lines of varying length.

beach gull: According to legend, gulls will only associate with a true recluse.

27 **integrity muddy or rinsed clean:** Allusion to a poem in *Mencius* (7.8) and "The Fisherman" chapter of *The Songs of Ch'u*. The poem describes a kind of recluse liberation in which muddy suggests a lack of integrity in government, causing social disorder; and clear suggests integrity in government, creating social order and prosperity.

> When Chill-Flood Creek flows clear
> I rinse my hat-strings clean.
> When Chill-Flood Creek flows muddy
> I rinse my feet clean.

30 **dark-enigma:** See Key Terms, p. 210.

36 **7th Moon, 14th Sun:** This calendrical format is often used. Here, it means "7th month, 14th day," but a literal translation of the original is used to give some sense of a more primal relation to the Cosmos that survived in high Chinese civilization. Indeed, the ideograms are pictographic images of *moon* and *sun*. And as noted before, the New Year in this lunar calendar comes twenty-one to fifty-one days after ours, and is thought to coincide with the beginning of spring. So, the 7th month is roughly equivalent to our August.

39 *Ch'i:* See Key Terms, p. 211.

40 **Studio:** Important spiritual/artistic worksites for artist-intellectuals, studios would typically have a library, work desk, calligraphy equipment, couch for relaxing, large windows for viewing landscape, etc. And because of their deep importance, studios were typically named, as here. Indeed, one studio particularly important in Yang's development was named by him Sincerity Studio, and Yang also took that as his literary name.

41 **gate:** Standard Ch'an image for the entrance to Ch'an awakening, and often appearing in Yang Wan-li's poems.

46   **Chuang Tzu's River . . . carefree-ease fish:** Chuang Tzu, seminal Taoist sage from the fourth century B.C.E., uses the term *carefree-ease* to describe fish joyfully drifting here and there in this river. For Chuang Tzu, *carefree ease* describes the joy of moving integral to earth and Cosmos as they unfurl effortlessly through their perennial transformations: an enlightened state that animals like those fish inhabit naturally, but that humans rarely master. This reference echoes through the Ch'an tradition as a principle dimension of enlightenment, appearing most prominently in *The Carefree-Ease Record* (see my translation by that title), one of the three classic collections of Ch'an sangha-cases (koans), composed in 1145, just as Yang Wan-li came of age.

57   **Traverse Mountain:** This site becomes a kind of philosophical way-station for Yang Wan-li. According to this poem, Yang has already passed by three times—and there are more passages to come, during which he will record his thoughts in poems: see pp. 100, 109, 146.

62   **Spirit-Vulture:** Spirit-Vulture Peak where, according to legend, the Ch'an tradition began when Buddha held up a flower and Mahakasyapa revealed his enlightenment by smiling.

65   **Wang Wei:** Seminal poet and painter of rivers-and-mountains landscape, for whom see my *The Selected Poems of Wang Wei* and *Wheel-Rim River.*

67   **No gates and no walls:** *No* here is 無, which is often used in Taoist/Ch'an philosophy for its rich double-meaning: "no" + "Absence." Read with this second meaning, the line becomes: "Absence gates and Absence walls, this ancient monastery . . ." For *Absence*, see Key Terms, p. 209. 無 is especially resonant here, because in Ch'an, gate is used philosophically to suggest "an entrance-way to insight." And only a few decades after this poem was written, one of the great sangha-case (koan) collections exploited this same double-meaning in its title: *No-Gate Gateway.*

68   **dragon:** See Key Terms, p. 211.

78 **It isn't headwinds . . . crag-bare peaks:** An alternate reading of this couplet suggests Ch'an's philosophical depths and that elemental eye at the heart of things:

> It isn't headwinds stopping us now. What origin-tissue
> am I seeing so utterly these ten thousand cragged peaks?

For more, see Introduction.

79 **and away. And they're everything I am:** Another reading of this line that adds more philosophical dimensions is "and away, my eye, and it's *ch'i*-weave mind."

80 **Heaven and earth:** Heaven and earth is an oft-used Chinese name for the Cosmos.

81 **Star River:** Our Milky Way.

100 **Traverse Mountain:** The numinous site that Yang visited numerous times, for which see p. 57 and note.

103 **link lines:** Poets often wrote poems together by taking turns writing lines following the rhymes and ideas of the other.

105 **Buddha-truth dragons:** In Ch'an storytelling, a black-dragon clutches the Buddha-truth pearl, and heroically raiding the dragon's lair and seizing that pearl is mythic description a of intense Ch'an practice leading to sudden enlightenment. This dragon clutching the pearl in its claws is the subject of many powerful paintings. For the dragon's significance more generally, see Key Terms, p. 211.

109 **Buddha face:** Reflecting the Ch'an doctrine that we are each, in our original-nature, Buddha.

110 **original-nature:** See Key Terms, p. 214.

114 **loom-of-origins:** A mythological description of Tao's generative process, the Cosmos in constant transformation, as a fabric that is woven out from a cosmic "loom-of-origins." Chuang Tzu, the seminal Taoist writer, describes it like this: "The ten thousand things all emerge from a loom-of-origins, and they all vanish back into it."

115 **white cloud:** This image of white cloud recurs often in the Chinese poetic tradition, simultaneously describing an empty and

free state of mind, the sense of secluded distances, and the sense of drifting free like a cloud.

119 **Linked Poem:** See note to p. 103.

122 **gate:** In Ch'an, the entranceway to enlightenment.

123 **great recluses:** It was said, with typical Ch'an irony, that a great recluse lives in the noisy city, while a small recluse lives in the quiet mountains.

124 **Iron-Flute:** Mythic flute made of solid iron and without mouthpiece or finger holes. In Ch'an legend, awakened masters could use it to make the soundless music of absolute insight. Hence, it became an image for enlightenment.

126 **door . . . gateway:** Literally "gate . . . gateway," where gateway is a locked gate or barrier that you can pass through or be blocked from passing through. In the Ch'an sense, this is the gateway to awakening. And indeed, this use of gate and gateway became central in *No-Gate Gateway*, the great sangha-case (koan) collection that appeared about forty years after this poem was written (for which, see my translation: *No-Gate Gateway*).

130 **breath-space seed-time:** 宇宙, a Chinese term for the Cosmos. Both ideograms contain the image for a roof at the top. Below that, 宇 has the image for breath spreading in the space beneath the roof, hence "breath-space home," and 宙 has the image for a seed sprouting beneath the roof, hence "seed-time home."

134 **Peony Hedge:** A reference to sangha-case #39 in *The Blue-Cliff Record*, entitled "Cloud-Gate's Peony Hedge" and beginning:

> A monk asked Cloud-Gate Mountain: "What is pure and clear dharma-nature?"
>
> "Peony hedge," replied Cloud-Gate.

135 ***Samadhi:*** In Indian Buddhism, *samadhi* simply meant "consciousness emptied of all subjective content," the goal of meditative practice. Taoism/Ch'an expands that meaning to include

empty-mind free of all conceptual structures, self dismantled completely, leaving consciousness open to its original-nature. See Key Terms, p. 214.

Wang An-shih: Major poet who lived the century before Yang Wan-li. Yang revered Wang An-shih (1021–1086) for his deep Ch'an insight and mastery of the quatrain form that Yang too preferred. Late in life, Wang An-shih lived within walking distance of Samadhi-Forest Monastery, which he adopted as a second home. He had a small residence at the monastery, which included his Words-Bright Library. For Wang's work, see my *The Late Poems of Wang An-shih*.

138   **Buddha-truth pearl:** See note to p. 105.

140   **lotus blossom:** Because its exquisite beauty is rooted in mud and murky water, the lotus blossom in conventional Buddhism is the image of pure Buddha-mind untainted by the world of compromise and struggle in which we live our everyday lives.

150   **Distinctions given up . . . :** Once we impose words and concepts and judgments on the tissue of empirical reality (here, the old masters detesting and Yang Wan-li loving mountains), reality becomes a mere object of thought: separated from us and no longer experienced in its own nature. At heart, Ch'an practice/awakening cultivates a form of dwelling in which mind and empirical reality are whole and integral, a single tissue—and this poem is Yang Wan-li's own version of that practice/awakening.

151   **Ox-Herding:** The Ch'an classic *Ten Ox-Herding Gathas and Pictures* tells of an ox-herd taming an ox, which represents the everyday mind with its wayward and unmanageable thoughts. It existed in numerous versions during the Sung Dynasty, earlier versions having fewer than ten episodes. This poem playfully dismantles the idea that Ch'an is a battle against the wandering thoughts that are clearly so natural to our minds.

152   **Dark-Moon Origin:** Literary name of Chu Hsi, one of the major intellectual figures of the Sung Dynasty.

158 **butterfly:** Echoing the famous butterfly story by Chuang Tzu (II.24), the seminal Taoist sage:

> Long ago, a certain Chuang Tzu dreamt he was a butterfly—a butterfly fluttering here and there, recognizing itself carefree on a whim, knowing nothing of Chuang Tzu. Then all of a sudden he woke to find that he was, beyond all doubt, Chuang Tzu. Who knows if it was Chuang Tzu dreaming a butterfly, or a butterfly dreaming Chuang Tzu? Chuang Tzu and butterfly: clearly there's a difference. This is called the transformation of things.

161 **sight's emptiest clarity:** See Key Terms, p. 213.

165 **three paths:** A recurring image in the recluse tradition, beginning eight centuries before this poem, when T'ao Ch'ien famously returned home to "three paths grown over." And when Wang An-shih retired to a reclusive life, he too made a point of having a garden with "three paths."

168 **9/9 Festival:** Dominated by thoughts of mortality, this autumn festival is celebrated on the 9th day of the 9th lunar month because the word for "9" is pronounced the same as the word meaning "long-lasting" or "long-living," hence "ever and ever." Hiking to mountaintops was a customary activity on this holiday, as was drinking chrysanthemum wine, which was playfully thought to promote long life.

170 **tiger . . . whiskers pulled:** Ch'an masters were often described as tigers, and to pull their whiskers was to challenge fearsome wildness, daring them to reveal their insight.
KHO-AAA!: This shout was a signature way that Ch'an masters revealed/taught Ch'an's deepest insight, which is outside of words and explanations.

171 **dragon . . . spring:** For dragon's role in the emergence of spring, see Key Terms, p. 211.

184 **Birthday of Humankind Born of Dragons:** Humans began as the offspring of Root-Breath and Lady She-Voice, dragons with

human heads, who emerged from Bright-Distance Mountain. In some tellings of the myth, Lady She-Voice gave birth to the world, and it was on the seventh day of this process that she gave birth to humankind. Hence, the birthday of humankind was celebrated on the seventh day of the new year, which in the Chinese calendar is the seventh day of spring.

Li Po: The great T'ang Dynasty poet (701–762 C.E.), much admired by Yang Wan-li and famed as a master of the same selfless spontaneity as these clouds billowing through mountains. For more, see my *The Selected Poems of Li Po*.

186 **where white clouds begin:** Clouds often seem to be rising off mountain landscape, so poets used the image to suggest that in high mountains they were wandering at a kind of origin place.

192 *adoration*: A rapturous experience of the wild rivers-and-mountains realm "mirrored" as a single overwhelming whole. Begun by Hsieh Ling-yün at the beginning of Ch'an and rivers-and-mountains poetry, cultivating adoration was a Ch'an practice leading to enlightenment.

195 **See Deep into Things Themselves:** This crucial concept dates back to Confucius and his *The Great Learning*, which describes it as the source of sage realization among the ancients:

> Wanting to rectify their minds, they began truing-up their thoughts. Wanting to true-up their thoughts, they began siting their understanding. And to site understanding is to see deep into things themselves.

gateway: See note to p. 126.

KEY TERMS

An Outline of Yang Wan-li's
Conceptual World

PRESENCE 有

The empirical universe, described in Taoist/Ch'an philosophy as the ten thousand things in constant transformation.

ABSENCE 無

The undifferentiated tissue of empirical reality, its ontological substrate infused mysteriously with a generative energy. It is "Absence" because it has no particular form. But because of its generative nature, it shapes itself into the individual forms of the Cosmos, then reshapes itself into other forms: the ten thousand things in the constant process of change. In fact, a more literal translation of 無 might be "formless," in contrast to "form-ful" for Presence. This ongoing generative process of Absence emerging into Presence is simply an ontological description of natural process, perhaps manifest most immediately in the seasonal cycle: the pregnant emptiness of Absence in winter, Presence's burgeoning forth in spring, the fullness of its flourishing in summer, and its dying back into Absence in autumn. Absence is known directly in meditation (widely practiced by ancient Chinese poets and intellectuals like Yang Wan-li), where it is experienced as empty consciousness itself, known in Ch'an terminology as "empty-mind" or "no-mind:" the formless generative source of thoughts.

Ref: 20, 39, 65, 91, 111, 127, 133, 156.

WAY (TAO) 道

Tao originally meant "way," as in "pathway" or "roadway," a meaning it has kept. But as the *Tao* of Taoism, it became the generative cosmological process of reality, an ontological "path *Way*" by which things come into existence, evolve through their lives, and then go out of existence, only to be transformed and reemerge in a new form: Absence emerging into Presence, Presence dissolving back into Absence. In practice, Way emphasizes the undifferentiated and generative nature of the existence-tissue, and is therefore nearly synonymous with Absence. Indeed, Lao Tzu describes it as "source" and "female" and "mother."

Ref: 190.

DARK-ENIGMA 玄

Dark-enigma is functionally equivalent to Absence, the generative ontological tissue from which the ten thousand things spring—but Absence before it is named. Or more properly, it is Way before it is named and conceptualized, before the concepts of Absence and Presence give birth to one another: existence without names and concepts, as it is in and of itself, the formless generative tissue where consciousness and the empirical Cosmos share their source.

Ref: 30, 39, 42, 50, 91, 127, 133, 170, 186.

ORIGIN-DARK QUIET 幽

Recurring often in Yang's poems, and in all Chinese recluse poetry, 幽 infuses the surface meaning "quiet solitude" with rich philosophical depths, beginning with the sense of "dark/secret/hidden/mystery."

And that leads finally to the term's deepest level, "origin-dark quiet." 幽 means forms, the ten thousand things, just on the not-yet-emergent side of the origin-moment: just as they are about to emerge from the formless ground of Absence, or just after they vanish back into that ground.

Ref: 4, 22, 103, 179, 198.

Сн'ı 氣

氣 is often described as the universal life-force breathing through things. But this presumes a dualism that separates reality into matter and a breath-force (spirit) that infuses it with life. Fully understood, *ch'i* is both breath-force and matter simultaneously. It is a single tissue generative through and through, the matter and energy of the Cosmos seen together as a single breath-force surging though its perpetual transformations. As such, it is virtually synonymous with Tao and Absence and dark-enigma, but emphasizing the existence-tissue's living dynamic nature.

Ref: 39, 55, 119.

DRAGON 龍

Dragon is a central mythical figure in the Chinese mind, and it recurs often in Yang Wan-li's poems. Feared and revered as the awesome force of change, of life itself, the dragon in ancient China was a mythological embodiment of Tao and its ten thousand things tumbling through their traceless transformations. Small as a silkworm and vast as all heaven and earth, dragon descends into deep waters in autumn, where it hibernates until spring, when its reawakening means the return of life to earth. It rises and ascends into sky, where it billows into thunderclouds and falls as spring's life-bringing rains. Its claws flash as lightning in those thunderclouds, and its rippling scales glisten in the bark of rain-soaked pines.

Ref: *passim.*

THUSNESS, ETC. 真

The sheer presence of reality in and of itself, free of our ideas and stories: reality experienced as sheer wonder and mystery, especially in its most magisterial form as rivers-and-mountains landscape. As such, it returns consciousness to empty-mind or mirror-mind, wherein "thusness-clarity" itself becomes the very content of consciousness or identity: a major dimension of awakening. This becomes clear in the etymological source of 真, which portrays an eye seeing straight: 𥃲. To capture this full range of connotations, a complete translation might be: "the wild thusness of things all clarity-absolute," and in context a range of translations emerge: "thusness," "sight-clarity-absolute," "thusness-clarity," "clarity-absolute."

Ref: *passim*.

EMPTY/EMPTINESS 空 AND 虚

These terms are often used in their ordinary sense, and by extension to mean "sky." But more philosophically, they are essentially synonymous with Absence, undifferentiated reality *empty* of individual forms, reality as a single formless and generative tissue to which we belong. Often used to describe consciousness emptied of all contents: Ch'an empty-mind (see below).

Ref: *passim*.

MIND 心
EMPTY-MIND 空心, 虚心

心 sometimes means "mind" in the common English sense of the word, as the center of language and thought and memory, the mental apparatus of identity. But generally in poetry and Ch'an, *mind* refers to consciousness emptied of all contents, a state reached through deep meditation: also confusingly called "empty-mind" or "no-mind" to distinguish it from *mind* in its conventional sense. And this empty-mind is nothing other than Absence, that generative cosmological tissue—for it is the empty source of thought and memory. In ancient China, there was no fundamental distinction between heart and mind: 心 connotes all that we think of in the two concepts together. In fact, the ideogram is a stylized version of the earlier 心, which is an image of the heart muscle, with its chambers at the locus of veins and arteries.

Ref: *passim.*

Eye/Sight/Looking 目，眼，見，直，etc., Mirror 鏡，鑑

In empty-mind, the act of perception becomes a spiritual act: empty-mind *mirroring* the world, making inside outside and outside inside. This is the heart of Ch'an as a landscape practice that shapes the imagistic texture of Chinese poetry. In such mirror-deep perception, earth's rivers-and-mountains landscape replaces thought and even identity itself, revealing the unity of consciousness and landscape/Cosmos that is the heart of sage dwelling for artist-intellectuals like Yang Wan-li. Here again, the eye at the very heart of things. Because the word for "empty-mind" (心) also means "heart," this mirror-deep seeing so crucial to Yang is not just a spiritual or intellectual experience, but also a rich emotional experience.

Ref: *passim.*

Idleness 閑，閒

Way unfurls its process of transformation in an effortless and spontaneous movement that can be described as idleness. Recognizing this, ancient China's artist-intellectuals and Ch'an adepts took living in idleness as a spiritual ideal, a kind of meditative wandering in which you move with the improvisational spontaneity of the Cosmos, but in everyday life within the gates of home, as is suggested in the etymology of the ideogram, connoting "profound serenity and quietness," its pictographic elements rendering a tree standing alone within the gates to a courtyard: 閑, combining two pictographic elements more clearly visible in their early forms as �門 (gate) and 𣎳 (tree, with its trunk, roots, and branches). Or in its alternate form, a moon shining through open gates: 閒, which replaces 𣎳 (tree) with ☽ (moon).

Ref: 11, 15, 39, 57, 171, 172, 175, 183.

WINE 酒

In Chinese poetry, the practice of wine often means drinking just enough wine to achieve a serene and selfless clarity of attention (the eye again), a state in which the isolation of a mind imposing distinctions on the world gives way to a sense of identity with the world. Alternately, getting wildly drunk was a liberation allowing one to move with the wild and selfless spontaneity of the Cosmos. Either way, wine was a lazy-bones Ch'an practice, a quick and pleasant way to enter a (temporary) enlightenment state. This is summarized in a pair of Yang's lines: "three cups and I've penetrated the vast Tao," and "three cups and I'm one with occurrence-appearing-of-itself" (*tzu-jan*: another near synonym for Tao's process).

Ref: *passim.*

ORIGINAL-NATURE 性

Prior to the definitions of self-identity, this is mind's original-nature as empty and mirror deep, selfless and integral to the existence-tissue Cosmos (Tao) and its ongoing transformations.

Ref: 110, 166, 169.

AWAKENING/ENLIGHTENMENT 悟 / 見性

An awakening to one's original-nature. That original-nature is empty-mind —and so, empty mirror-deep seeing is itself tantamount to awakening.

Indeed, one term for enlightenment is 見性, which is often read as: "see" + "original-nature." But it might also be read "the original-nature of seeing," and 見 actually contains a pictographic image of that elemental eye at the heart of things: 目 , which appears in early forms as 𥄀 . That original-nature is unborn and empty and is in fact Way or Absence itself. And so, awakening/enlightenment is, in addition to dwelling as empty-mind, a selfless "wandering boundless and free" through the selfless transformations of Way's vast and ongoing process. These two aspects of this enlightenment define the form of Yang Wan-li's poetry. First is the immediate experience of empty-mind mirroring of thusness itself, a mirroring in which reality becomes the content of mind and identity and that is manifest in the imagistic texture typical of Chinese poetry like Yang's. The second aspect is selfless and spontaneous movement "wandering boundless and free" and integral to the Cosmos (Tao) unfurling through its perpetual transformations, which is manifest in the improvisational structure of Yang's poetry (see Introduction, p. xviii f.).

Ref: passim.

FINDING LIST

Location of Poems in the Original Texts

1. 楊萬里集箋校 (*Yang Wan-li Chi Chien Chiao*): Page number.
2. 誠齋詩集 (*Ch'eng Chai Shih Chi*) SPPY: *Chüan*, page number, leaf.

PAGE	1. 楊萬里集箋校	2. 誠齋詩集
3	32	1.5b
4	17	1.3a
4	23	1.4a
5	23	1.4a
6	92	2.4a
6	125	2.9b
7	104	2.6a
9	156	3.3b
10	159	3.4b
10	186	3.10a
11	189	3.10b
11	200	4.1b
12	198	4.1a
13	217	4.3b

PAGE	1. 楊萬里集箋校	2. 誠齋詩集
13	227	4.5a
14	236	4.6b
14	239	4.7b
15	249	4.9a
15	321	6.5a
16	242	4.8a
17	247	4.9a
18	255	4.10a
19	284	5.5b
20	286	5.6a
21	286	5.6a
22	302	6.2a
23	341	6.7b
23	373	7.5a
24		
25	330	6.6b
26	374	7.5a
26	397	7.9a
27	396	7.8b
28	407	8.2b
29	408	8.2b
29	408	8.2b
30	412	8.3b
31	418	8.5a
35	441	9.1a
35	444	9.1b
36	451	9.2a

Page	1. 楊萬里集箋校	2. 誠齋詩集
36	462	9.4a
37	471	9.5b
37	483	9.7b
38	499	10.4a
39	501	10.4b
40	503	10.4b
41	517	11.1a
41	528	11.3a
42	508	10.6a
44	554	11.9a
45	549	11.7b
45	572	12.3a
46	573	12.3a
46	574	12.3a
47	575	12.3b
48	584	12.5b
49	586	12.6a
50	586	12.6a
51	588	12.6b
51	588	12.6b
52	589	12.7a
52	593	12.7b
53	595	12.8a
53	596	12.8a
54	599	12.8b
54	616	13.4b
55	619	13.5a

PAGE	1. 楊萬里集箋校	2. 誠齋詩集
56	624	13.6a
57	647	14.1b
57	666	14.4b
58	647	14.1b
59	663	14.4a
60	673	14.5b
61	676	14.6a
61	683	14.7b
62	684	14.7b
63	701	15.2b
64	703	15.3b
65	704	15.3b
65	715	15.6a
66	705	15.4a
67	717	15.6b
67	745	16.2a
68	748	16.2b
68	749	16.2b
69	753	16.3a
70	762	16.4b
71	764	16.4b
71	768	16.5a
72	770	16.5b
73	771	16.5b
73	780	16.7a
74	780	16.7a
75	780	16.7a

PAGE	1. 楊萬里集箋校	2. 誠齋詩集
76	801	17.3b
76	811	18.1a
77	813	18.1a
78	821	18.2b
78	870	19.6a
79	823	18.3a
80	829	18.4b
81	847	19.2a
82	876	19.7a
83	881	19.8a
83	928	20.7b
84	897	20.1a
85	903	20.2b
86	913	20.4a
87	919	20.5a
89	924	20.6a
90	925	20.6b
91	926	20.7a
93	929	20.7b
93	944	21.1b
94	983	21.8a
95	958	21.4a
95	997	21.10b
96	1137	24.7a
97	1142	24.8b
98	1141	24.8b
98	1244	27.1b

PAGE	1. 楊萬里集箋校	2. 誠齋詩集
99	1246	27.2a
100	1248	27.2b
101	1248	27.2b
101	1251	27.3a
102	1271	27.6b
105	1296	27.11a
105	1322	28.4a
106	1327	28.5a
106	1329	28.5b
107	1328	28.5b
108	1346	28.8b
109	1357	28.10b
110	1330	28.6a
110	1358	28.11a
111	1363	28.12a
112	1364	28.12a
113	1365	28.12b
115	1366	28.12b
115	1366	28.12b
116	1376	29.1a
116	1382	29.2a
117	1392	29.3b
118	1386	29.3a
118	1449	30.6a
119	1450	30.6a
120	1464	30.9a
126	1484	31.3b

PAGE	1. 楊萬里集箋校	2. 誠齋詩集
128	1495	31.6b
129	1499	31.8a
130	1509	32.1a
135	1607	33.6a
135	1613	33.7a
136	1627	33.9b
138	1647	34.3b
138	1650	34.4a
139	1655	34.5a
140	1665	34.8a
141	1672	34.8b
142		34.9b
143	1683	34.10b
144	1700	35.2a
144	1714	35.4b
145	1708	35.3a
146	1725	35.6a
147	1746	35.10b
148	1747	35.10b
148	1763	36.1a
149	1754	35.11b
150	1754	35.12a
151	1755	35.12a
152	1765	36.1a
152	1778	36.3b
153	1766	36.1b
154	1769	36.1b

PAGE	1. 楊萬里集箋校	2. 誠齋詩集
155	1793	36.6a
156	1796	36.6b
157	1799	36.7a
161	1828	35.12b
161	1829	36.12b
165	1843	37.1b
165	1846	37.2a
166	1846	37.2b
167	1847	37.2b
167	1879	37.7b
168	1885	37.8b
169	1886	37.9a
170	1888	37.9b
171	1893	37.10a
172	1903	38.1b
172	1920	38.5a
173	1921	38.5a
173	1928	38.6b
174	1943	38.9b
175	1959	39.1b
176	2004	39.8b
177	2041	40.4b
178	2063	40.7b
179	2074	40.9a
180	2087	40.11a
181	2097	40.12b
182	2102	40.13b

Page	1. 楊萬里集箋校	2. 誠齋詩集
183	2103	40.13b
183	2111	41.2a
184	2112	41.2a
184	2123	41.4a
185	2137	41.5a
185	2159	41.9a
186	2161	41.9b
187	2165	41.10b
187	2194	42.3a
188	2183	42.1a
189	2196	42.3b
190	2213	42.6b
191	2214	42.7a
192	2215	42.7a
193	2216	42.7b
194	2225	42.9a
194	2237	42.11a
195	2236	42.10b
196	2240	42.11b
198	2242	42.12a

ABOUT DAVID HINTON

DAVID HINTON has published numerous books of poetry and essays, and many translations of ancient Chinese poetry and philosophy that create contemporary works of compelling literary power that also convey the actual texture and density of the originals. This work has earned wide acclaim and many national awards, including a Guggenheim Fellowship and both of the major awards given for poetry translation in the United States: the Landon Translation Award (Academy of American Poets) and the PEN American Translation Award. Most recently, Hinton received a lifetime achievement award from the American Academy of Arts and Letters.